LEARNING TO MANAGE YOUR CAREER IN A TURBULENT AND CHANGING WORLD

LEARNING TO FLY: HOW TO MANAGE YOUR CAREER IN A TURBULENT AND CHANGING WORLD

MIKE ROSENBERG

ANTHEM PRESS

Anthem Press

An imprint of Wimbledon Publishing Company
www.anthempress.com

This edition first published in UK and USA 2022

by ANTHEM PRESS
75–76 Blackfriars Road, London SE1 8HA, UK
or PO Box 9779, London SW19 7ZG, UK
and
244 Madison Ave #116, New York, NY 10016, USA

British Library Cataloguing-in-Publication Data
A catalogue record for this book is available from the British Library.

Library of Congress Control Number: 2022932212
A catalog record for this book has been requested.

ISBN-13: 978-1-83998-510-2 (Pbk)
ISBN-10: 1-83998-510-0 (Pbk)

This title is also available as an e-book.

To the thousands of students, friends and business people who have shared their stories with me over the years and to Paddy Miller who was my teacher, role model, mentor, and friend.

CONTENTS

FOREWORD

We are now in the midst of what some call "the Decisive Decade" in that the global climate change trajectory for the planet will be set by the actions we take in the coming years. In the last 20 years, technology has created the so-called Fourth Industrial Revolution altering how we work and live. COVID-19 has revealed our very real risk of global pandemics, exposed deficiencies in public health systems and provided a test case for technology and new ways of working. As if that wasn't sufficient challenge, national and global politics are under tremendous strain, with fissures within our countries and between them getting wider. Civil discourse is threatened, democracy is under threat, and capitalism is being questioned. Recent surveys show that trust in virtually all institutions is at historically low levels. Yet at the same time, people across the world are looking to business to address these myriad problems. And in surveys, the most trusted institutions are indeed "my employer."

Against this backdrop, how should we make sensible career choices and select "my employer?" The organizations for which we work not only have to produce products and profits, but increasingly are being asked to do much more. Which means that we may be asked to do more. And looking forward, organizations will almost surely do their work in new ways. As will we. So as the world becomes more complex, our career journeys—increasingly longer lived as life expectancy increases—will become more rich and varied. Historical career advise may not be relevant in the new world that is emerging.

This guide is written for today's career traveler trying to not only navigate their own uncertain future, but also do this while the world is changing. At the core of any advice book is the advisor, the writer offering guidance for readers. Professor Mike Rosenberg, author of this guide to career management in turbulent and changing world, forthrightly warns readers of career books to be aware of the biases that readers might encounter: "The only thing to watch out for is that these books tend to tell the author's story and may not be objective."

Throughout this helpful and timely guide, we encounter Mike on nearly every page—and benefit from his focus on the future. We learn about and from his own career journey, from engineer to consultant to search executive to professor, as well as his values and beliefs. We learn about and from his family, his friends, his colleagues, his mentors, and his many students. We learn about and from the wide range of books and articles he summarizes and synthesizes on our behalf. Because his daily work is not in career counseling, we get practical advice from someone who has been on both sides of the hiring fence—and as a search consultant, been a gatekeeper.

But most importantly, we are guided by an advisor who has been researching the trends which will shape the future, including geopolitics and climate. We can benefit from his macro long-horizon perspective on sectors and skill sets. Throughout, he provides the well-considered, fact-based, but authentic advice we might receive from a trusted friend or colleague more attuned to humble than humblebrag tendencies. And someone who focuses more on the future than on the past.

The guide straddles paradoxical perspectives. While it is focused on the individual job seeker, it is keenly attuned to those employing them. For example, the section of the book on search and selection consultants, presented in a matter-of-fact fashion, provides the reader with useful and frank insights on what headhunters do and don't do. While readers will likely be fixated on the next step in their career, the book has them think about the entire journey. And in thinking about that future, Mike takes a very wide gauge, willing to venture a guess on which parts of our economies and societies will require skills in the future—and where there are likely more opportunities.

The structure of the book is disarmingly simple. It begins by asking the reader "What are your experiences, passions and constraints?" What do you have to offer—mind, heart and hands? But the core of the book focuses on three key aspects of our careers that define our destinations: space, role and place. Space is the "field of endeavour"—think of it as sector, industry or field. Role reflects the nature of the contribution you can make. And place means the city or region where you would call home.

"Space" sounds overly simplistic, but Mike nudges us from thinking about traditional industrial or sectoral definitions to reframe our thinking about the problems we seek to solve. He concludes the chapter with a list of ten "spaces" that he thinks will likely need considerable brainpower, and hence offer great opportunities, including clean energy, health care, clean mobility, manufacturing 4.0, sustainable consumption and more.

"Roles" are far more fluid in a world that embraces digital technologies as well as post-COVID changes in ways of working. Roles encompass a set of skills, attitudes, and functions. The guide is peppered with experiences that remind us of the importance of role. For example, Mike shared a story of introducing a student who was passionate about climate change with a CEO of a carbon credit trading firm. While the intellectual fit was great, the connection didn't work, because the student didn't like any of the roles—the work to be done. Again, adopting a forward-looking approach, Mike offers ten possible roles that will continue to add value in the future, including marketeer, systems engineer, salesperson, supply chain expert, human resource manager, entrepreneur and others.

"Place" seems outdated in our virtual world, but remains important, both at the firm and individual level. Despite digital leveling, the world's largest cities remain the centers for economic growth. Clusters such as Silicon Valley, Alley Fen and others are real. And place matters personally, as vividly exemplified by the author, whose thoughtful comments come from the vantage point of someone born to American parents in London, studied in New York and Boston and Michigan, then who moved Spain for the past 30 years but travels internationally extensively. Much of this chapter is a clear-eyed reflection on the likely future connections between place and technology, post-COVID work patterns, commuting, business travel, ex-patriation, and telecommuting, but with the critical observation that place is likely the most important determinant of the quality of your life.

Given Mike's extensive experience and work with career travelers at all stages, it's not surprising that the guide has sections addressing different phases of life, from finding the right combination of space-role-place, to changing jobs, to changing phases—and the north star, finding purpose. Throughout, Mike weaves together the tales of many individuals, data, research and his own interpretations in a fashion that is readable and useful and always future facing.

There is no one-size-fits-all set of prescriptions for career advice, yet without a point of view, "it depends" is the unsatisfactory answer. The point of view here comes from Professor Rosenberg, who reminds us that advise and advisor are intertwined. His perspective is clearly informed by his experience in business and business school. His perspective is also grounded in his life experiences as an American ex-patriate with a global perspective. Finally—and perhaps most critically, his perspective is rooted in his work as an academic who contemplates future trends.

Some might not resonate with the particular examples that he offers up for consideration or identify with the global or long horizon perspective he takes. You might violently disagree with his characterization of discrimination as sometimes the result of "cold business logic" and the need for a thick skin. But throughout, readers can be assured of a thoughtful, forward looking, caring perspective. Books of this sort don't earn the kudos of academia, nor are they garunteed to be best sellers. They can, however, help people in the complex journey of their careers, much in the same way that dedicated educators do. Were you to stop by Prof. Rosenberg's office hours and ask for advice, I suspect you'd get an abbreviated version of this guide. It is a "master class," offered by a master teacher and futurist, as an extra gift to his students—and now to all. We are better able to plan our future because we understand ourselves better—and have a greater understanding for the complicated future world that lies ahead.

INTRODUCTION

Russia's invasion of Ukraine is just the latest example that the world is in constant flux and why people might want to look ahead when thinking about what to do with their professional careers.

Covid 19 is another example. In March 2020, I had been scheduled to teach a group of executives in Shanghai, and I remember my sister asking me on New Year's Eve if it would be a good idea considering the virus that had broken out in Wuhan, a city about 500 miles up the Yangtze River. I had not heard about the virus up until that point and, like most people, had no idea of what was about to happen. We ended up moving the event to New York City but actually cancelled it just after I arrived in New York.

At IESE's building in New York, my colleagues and I decided to do a webinar on the unfolding situation for the people who were supposed to have come in for the course as well as open it up to other people who might be interested.

One thing led to another, and IESE Business School eventually aired 45 webinars as a way of helping the international business community cope with the crisis. I moderated about half of the webinars and was the academic director of the series.

This experience gave me access to a wide range of thought leaders, academicians and businesspeople as they managed the global pandemic, which would go on to infect more than 500 million and kill more than 6 million people all over the world.

While I was in New York I also met with several publishers about a manuscript which I had been working on to capture everything I had learned about managing careers and getting new jobs as a result of my experience as a management consultant, headhunter and business school professor.

As the COVID crisis unfolded, however, I decided not to publish the book as much of that early draft was already out of date. The pandemic has changed the business landscape and the world of work beyond recognition.

As the world slowly comes out of the Covid crisis and deals with the knock on effects of Russia's invasion of Ukraine, we can begin to see some of the key aspects of the new normal and I felt it was time to go ahead with the project.

An uncertain future

Perhaps the biggest lesson that we can all take away from the last couple of years is that the future is fundamentally uncertain. Although virologists, public health experts and even Bill Gates have been talking about the world's lack of preparation for a major outbreak for some time, no one really saw Covid coming. In a similar way, even though many people discussed how Russia was unhappy with NATO's expansion to the East, we were still surpised by the invasion when it began in March, 2022.

In terms of career management, each of us have three possible choices to make when faced with an uncertain and changing world.

The first choice is to do nothing. This is perhaps the easiest course although it might take some effort to ignore what is happening around you. In making this choice you assume that things will stay the same or at least will do so long enough to "make it through."

If, after thinking deeply about it, you come to the conclusion that your own life will not be turned upside down and choose to continue with what you have been doing, then your choice makes sense to me.

If, on the other hand, you choose not to really think about the future or enter into denial about what is going on around you, then I find that inaction to be somewhat irresponsible especially if you have a family to take care of or other responsibilities.

A second option is to wait and see what happens and then to be ready to react to change when it comes. The idea here is not to panic and jump into the future before being very sure what change will be real and what might be illusory. You might, for example, start learning the basics of coding or study Mandarin just to be ready for a more digital and/or Chinese centric world.

A third choice is to develop a view and act on it right away. This can be both rewarding and exciting but depends on either being right about the future or being so passionate about something that it almost does not matter.

Being right is not only about what will happen in the world but also in terms of when. Sometimes, for example, what seems to be the next big thing turns out not to be, and spending a significant portion of your professional life on a business model or a technology which does not make it can be emotionally and financially draining.

A slightly different approach is to pursue a path that is so close to your heart that it almost does not matter what happens next because you would not want to do anything else no matter what.

What to do?

In meetings with people about their professional future, I always ask what they want to do and find they typically react in one of a number of ways.

Some people answer in a way which is genuine but often not terribly useful in terms of job hunting or career planning. They might say I want to work with people, travel or find a good work–life balance.

Other answers have to do with finding the right kind of environment such as a small or large company with a certain kind of culture or style. Many people have only figured out what they do not want to do which is at least a good start.

People who have recently lost their job and many MBA students say they are open to many things or even anything. While this response may be true in some cases, it is very difficult to help someone who does not know what they want. If you do not know what you are looking for it seems to me that you will probably never find it.

What people who want to make a change often believe is that by not choosing a course they keep their options open. In my experience most people are reluctant to choose, but for different reasons.

There are a small number of people who are genuinely open to different types of work, different industries and even living in different parts of the world. They are like the people who shop for last-minute holidays and go to the airport not knowing where they will end up. This is o.k. as long as you really do not mind what you do or where you do it.

There are also people who do know what they would love to do but have given up on it as unrealistic. They then shut down what is in their hearts and start looking for "a job." I question the probability of success if one is pursuing a course which goes against their personal desires and ambitions.

A third group of people truly do not know what they want to do and have trouble choosing between a wide variety of seemingly interesting options. I believe that people are capable of doing almost anything but also feel strongly that we cannot do everything at once and that potential employers will be reluctant to give us a chance to do something we have never done before and for which they see that we have no significant qualifications or interest.

There are, finally, people who hold back from making a clear choice because they think that by not choosing they will increase their chances of finding the job they need. What these people are saying is that they need a job more than a career path.

In my experience this last idea is mistaken for three reasons. One reason it does not work is that nobody will hire you if you show little interest in the job, industry or mission of the organization in question and true interest is hard to fake.

The second reason that keeping one's options open does not work is that it leads to dividing your efforts among different ideas and losing focus. Time and energy are finite resources, and it is a bad idea to spread them too thin.

The third reason to choose is that intention can be a powerful tool. Deepak Chopra writes about how intention leads to what he calls synchronicity, and we may open our eyes to possibilities that we would otherwise not be able to see only when we are focused and committed.

How to choose?

This book is written to assist you in charting a professional path through the changing world we live in.

Chapter 1 discusses how the world is changing at an ever-increasing pace. Besides the pandemic and its consequences, the chapter discusses the unfolding geopolitical situation, the impact that digitalization and automation is having on the future of work and the steadily eroding situation concerning the natural environment.

The next chapter provides a conceptual framework for figuring out what to do. This includes your *experience, passions* and the *constraints* you have in your life. Putting these three ideas together will allow you to figure out which way to go.

That involves choosing in which *space*, or field of endeavor, you should seek to work, the *role* you choose to play and the *place* meaning the region or city in which you intend to live.

Before thinking too deeply about what to do next, it is very important to develop a good understanding of what we have done before and being able to tell your personal story.

To help you with this, I find two metaphors to be helpful, and Chapter 3 discusses each in depth as well as discussing how to develop scenarios for the future.

The next few chapters then drill down into the ideas of *space*, *role* and *place* and discuss how you can think about them in isolation. Chapter 7 is then about building combinations which make sense both today and tomorrow and balance your interests with more practical issues such as paying the rent. Chapter 8 discusses the challenges associated with changing jobs such as the pain and anguish that can sometimes be felt when we lose a job and how to go through the process of getting a new one.

Your professional life will probably go through a process of evolution during which different jobs make up a series of different phases. Chapter 9 discusses challenges associated with changing these broader phases.

Chapter 10 discusses the importance of education and training in the context of managing a professional career and provides a set of criteria with which to evaluate specific options.

Chapter 11 then goes on to a discussion of values and purpose and the importance of feeling that our personal life and work add up to something with meaning. Chapter 12 summarizes the themes in the book and also offers a set of forms and charts with which to apply these concepts to your own situation.

This is a personal book as it represents personal impressions and ideas I use in discussions with people about important, personal decisions. Many of the stories will also come from students and participants in programs at IESE Business School as much of my personal experience has been shaped in the institution.

Where I have borrowed ideas from other people, I will attempt to give them full credit, and if I forget someone please do not take it to heart as the error was completely unintentional.

Barcelona, April 2022

CHAPTER 1

UNDERSTANDING THE WORLD

The idea that the world is changing at an increasingly faster pace has become something of a cliché over the last 10–20 years. Having graduated from college and business schools in the 1980s, I lived through the last 30 years and actually did not observe the changes to be so dramatic as they were happening.

In hindsight, it is clear today that small changes added up and things are very different today than they were when I was younger. This was already true before the virus upended many of our lives in March 2019 and brought about an incredible time of very rapid transformation. Two years later the war in Ukrane has started a similar process.

In this context, my advice is to expand your thinking about your next job by really trying to understand the world before figuring out where you want to fit into it professionally.

The good news is that if we put aside the impact of the virus and the war, we are living at the most prosperous time in history. In my lifetime, the global population has more than doubled and world GDP has increased about 15 times in terms of constant dollars. As a whole, we are wealthier than ever and live better, longer and possibly even more meaningful lives.

Of course, the virus has killed more than 6 million people, reduced economic output on a global level by 6–7 percent in 2020 and placed an unequal hardship on the world's poor as well as older people, families with less living space and many others.

Even before the pandemic, globalization had left many people behind both in the industrial economies and the developing world, and there are still hundreds of millions of people living in dire poverty.

In a similar way, the war had upended the lives of millions of people. Besides the possibility of more pandemics, the world faces issues related to air and water pollution, as well as the consequences of climate change, fractious politics and geopolitical conflict and a number of other social and economic issues such as rising inequality.

At the same time, while potentially transformative digital technologies offer promise and hope for many of the problems facing the world, they also cause disruption to industries, companies and individuals making things more unequal.

The one thing we can be sure of is that the future will be different from today.

The Pandemic and Its Impact

This last period of rapid globalization is often compared to the late 1800s and early 1900s when the world went through a similar process of economic expansion. This phase of globalization came to a roaring stop as a result of the First World War and the subsequent pandemic known as the Spanish Flu. That virus, which swept the world between 1918 and 1919, infected approximately 500 million people and killed an estimated 20–50 million people.

Before Covid 19, there have been outbreaks of different strains of influenza that reached global proportions in 1957 and 1968.[1] Additional outbreaks include SARS in 2003 and MERS in 2012. The more global the world is, the more people will travel helping such viruses to spread.

The good news is that medical science has been advancing at an amazing pace, and by and large the world can manage infectious diseases. In his 2015 book *Homo Deus*, Yuval Harari wrote about our ability to defeat disease as one of the signs that humanity was entering a new chapter in its existence.

This pandemic shows that Harari was half right. COVID-19 has provided a showcase of our scientific capabilities in terms of testing and vaccines but still demonstrated that we are far from conquering disease.

An aging world

The starting point for a discussion of health and health care is that people are living much longer lives. In 1950 the average life expectancy was 45.5 years for the world as a whole or more than 70 for Norway and other wealthy countries.[2]

---

1   E. D. Kilbourne, "Influenza Pandemics of the 20th Century." *Emerging Infectious Diseases* 12, no. 1 (2006): 9–14. https://doi.org/10.3201/eid1201.051254.
2   United Nations, World Population Prospects 2019.

Today, the world average is almost 73 years and people live well past 80 in the world's richest countries.

COVID-19 is much more dangerous for older people than for the rest of the population partly because they also suffer from hearing loss, cataracts, arthritis, respiratory ailments, cancer, dementia and other maladies.

A separate trend is that women are choosing to have fewer babies around the world due to higher income levels and other factors adding to a rise in the percentage of older people in many countries. This trend is particularly high in Japan, Northern Europe and North America.

An aging population can be seen as a human success story but, like everything else, causes problems including an increase in the percentage of older people and a decrease in the percentage of younger people in the workforce. One issue is that most public pension systems work on the assumption that younger workers will pay for the benefits of retired people. If there are not enough workers, then the systems will collapse.

Technology and access

Over the last 50–70 years, medical science and technology have made enormous advances. The accelerated development of vaccines for the virus is just an example of this progress.

Today we have sensors and scanners to "see" inside the body, chemical and biological treatments for most diseases and a wide array of tools and devices that can be used in surgeries around the world and also in people's homes to give them a better life.

Going even further, scientists are now beginning to understand how our bodies work at the cellular level and may, one day, find ways to stop the aging process itself.

The problem is that all of this development comes with a cost. The United States, for example, spent on the order of $ 4 trillion on health care in 2020 or about 20 percent of its GDP. Globally, the world spends more than twice that amount or about 10 percent of the total world economy, and this is without a full accounting of the costs associated with the pandemic.

Different countries have taken different paths to manage and deploy health care, although generally speaking there is more care available for wealthier countries than poorer ones. The United States, for example, has an incredibly complex, decentralized and mainly private health care system.

Despite having some of the best medical facilities in the world, the system in the United States showed many of its weaknesses during the pandemic. For example, it took the country months to roll out testing capabilities, there was overcrowding in hospitals and vaccine distribution initially lagged behind the government's original schedule.

Other countries with well-developed public health systems appear to have been better able to coordinate policies, share best practices and move resources from place to place as needed. At another extreme, many poorer countries have not been able to respond adequately to the pandemic as it stretched their public health systems beyond capacity.

The great resignation

One impact of the pandemic and the measures put in place to control its spread is that more people quit their jobs in the period from November 2020 to October 2021 than would normally do so. For the 12-month period about 5 million more people quit their jobs than in a similar period two years before according to the Bureau of Labor Statistics tracks which tracks the percentage of people who quit their jobs based on a monthly survey. Similar numbers are coming out of the UK and other advanced economies.

People are always quitting jobs so it is important to compare the rate after the pandemic to what came before in April 2019, for example, 3,992,000 are estimated to have quit their jobs or 2.8 percent of the US workforce. The same statistic for April 2018 was 2.3 percent so the difference is 0.5 percent or about 700,000 people.

In looking through the different articles and reports the reasons for the mass resignation include the following:

- People being burned out by zoom meetings and working from home;
- Others and especially frontline personnel like nurses and checkout people concerned about their own health;
- People who feel that their wages and benefits are simply too low or limited to justify the time spent at work.

At the more granular level, the quit rates in health care, retail and food service are all up by a full percentage point or more compared to a couple of years ago, and these are some of the lowest-paid and highest-risk sectors of the economy.

In his opinion piece on the subject in *The New York Times*, Paul Krugman lends his support to the ideas of Arindrajit Dube, from the University of Massachusetts, who thinks it is due to people quitting jobs they didn't like anyway.

One thing I have heard from many people from all over the world is that the pandemic has helped them remember what is most important in life such as health and family. My opinion is that at least some of these five million people realized in 2020 that their current work was taking them away from that without providing enough economic compensation or a sense of purpose to make that sacrifice worthwhile. Krugman later changed his view of these numbers as people came back to work after the pandemic began to pass. I do think, however, that he was right the first time and Covid-19 has given us a glimpese of a trend which might become more important over time.

Other implications

In terms of career planning, the first point to take away from this discussion of health care is the opportunities involved in developing the science and technology and deploying it to the people who need it.

The health care industry is also going through a profound digital transformation, and this will create tremendous opportunities for some people while creating difficult challenges for others.

The second is the link between access to health care and where you choose to live and work in the world. The advantage of public systems such as the one they have in Canada, England, or Spain is that you can get treatment for pretty much anything without going into debt. The disadvantage is that while such systems are usually fantastic at primary care, they can be overstretched for advanced procedures with long backlogs and waiting periods.

The third aspect to consider is that most experts believe that Covid 19 is not the last virus that will sweep across the world in your lifetime.

Geopolitics

The second issue which needs to be considered is geopolitical uncertainty around the world as shown much too clearly by Russia's invasion of Ukriane. These tensions arise from the collapse of the Soviet Union and the rise of China as a player on the world stage.

Peace and prosperity are essential preconditions for human development, and there will be serious problems in different parts of the world over the course of the next 5 to 50 years.

Understanding what is going on in the part of the world you live in or do business with is increasingly important as the world becomes increasingly complex. The good news is that geopolitical conflicts do not happen overnight. They are the result of historical trends, economic and political rivalry and political movements. As such they can be studied, analyzed and in some cases predicted. Russia's invasion of Ukraine is a case in point.

The difficulty in doing such analysis is that most people in business did not study history or geopolitics in college and feel that these issues are beyond them. My opinion is that if you spend some time on it, you can acquire a working knowledge of the issues faced by the parts of the world that you are most interested in. The framework I developed for this purpose looks at the geopolitical situation of a country or region in terms of three ideas which are loosely based on accounting principles.

The *fixed aspects* include the location of a country, its history and topography, endowment of natural resources, and so on.

S*emifixed aspects* are those that will most likely endure for many years but will change during the course of history. The democratic system of government in the United States, for example, is unlikely to change in the next 50–100 years but is a relatively recent phenomena in historical terms. Even more recent is the European Union (EU) in its current form. The EU is, however, still evolving adding countries in the east on the one hand and dealing with the implications of the UK's leaving on the other.

Current aspects are those which will play out over five years. Such aspects usually include the current election cycle or trending issues in civil society and the media.

I will discuss four examples of geopolitical issues that have come up in the last few years in order to illustrate this idea even though I urge you to do your own analysis based on the parts of the world you are interested in and when you are reading this book.

These examples are about events which have been relevant at the beginning of the 2020s and may be less applicable to your reality.

The future of Europe

The UK's vote to leave the EU in 2016, for example, started a long period of negotiation and uncertainty that has upended the lives of hundreds of thousands of people who had assumed that such a thing could never happen.

As this book goes to press many of the details are still being worked out between the Irish Republic and the six counties of Northern Ireland. The broader issue is the future of the EU itself and if other countries will follow the UK's example.

Russia's Western border.

Another issue in Europe is the war in Ukriane. Since the ouster of Victor Yanucovish and Russia's illegal annexation of The Crimea in 2014, Russia and Ukraine have been in conflict in the Eastern part of the country. The invasion is in may ways, the logical escalation of that conflict.

The deeper issue is what will be the relationship between Europe and Russia as time goes by. Europe still needs Russian gas, especially in the northeast. The Russian government, however, is deeply suspicious of the West and sees the expansion of the North Atlantic Treaty Organization to the Baltic States as a provocation.

The Middle East

Israel's recent recognition by the United Arab Emirates, Bahrain, Sudan and Morocco in 2021 may represent a watershed movement in terms of Israel's diplomatic isolation in the area which has been a semifixed aspect of its situation for many years.

In my view, however, the biggest threat to the region is the rivalry between Shia Iran and Sunni Saudi Arabia. Many analysts see the war in Yemen as a precursor to an eventual fight between the two largest countries in the region. Iran has the bigger army, but Saudi Arabia spent more on armaments than any country except the United States and China in 2019.

For almost 25 years, shipping in the Persian/Arabian Gulf has been protected by the American fifth fleet which is based in Bahrain. The American presence is thought to act as a deterrent to any instigation on the part of Iran. An important question is if the United States will maintain the fleet in the Gulf forever given the fact that it no longer imports much oil from the region.

China and the United States

Probably the most pressing issue faced by the world is the increasing tension between China and the United States which mainly has to do with trade but also with industrial espionage. According to Niall Ferguson, an historian who teaches at Stanford, we are already in Cold War 2.0 between the United States and China.

On the eastern side of China there is another potential flash point in the South China Sea which, like Taiwan, China claims as its own. China has not condemned Russia's invasion of Ukraine and may expect Russian support should it move on Taiwan.

Part of China's strategy is the one belt, one road initiative which involves financing infrastructure projects across the region in exchange for political support and access to markets for Chinese companies. The idea is to create a semifixed commercial and logistical networking firmly binding many of the countries in the region to China.

Implications

The geopolitical situation affects patterns of international trade even when things are relatively calm. When war does break out, it not only causes death and destruction but also has a devastating impact on the economy wiping out savings, ruining careers, and so on.

Far short of war, however, there are a number of geopolitical issues which can affect your daily life. Tensions between countries, the introduction of new tariffs or economic sanctions and even terrorist acts can all make life more difficult.

Clearly the biggest implication of geopolitical change has to do with the choice you make about where in the world you live and work.

Living in a highly politicized and polarized environment can also take its toll in terms of overall levels of stress. A difficult and acrimonious political situation can also sometimes freeze investment and put an overall brake on economic activity.

Geopolitical tension also has an impact on different businesses. The threat of war naturally stimulates spending in defense industries but, on the other hand, will devastate a regions' tourism business to name just a couple of simple examples.

Digitalization and Automation

A third issue which will impact the future of the job market is digitalization, automation and the massive introduction of artificial intelligence (AI). All this has been greatly enabled by the introduction of 5G and has been accelerated by the pandemic and the world's reaction to it.

Digitalization in its broadest sense is the process of using computers and digital telecommunications networks to do just about anything that lends itself to their use. The impact of using digital technology can alter the fundamental economics of many businesses with enormous consequences.

Automation is the replacement of human labor by machines, and this has been going on since the dawn of the Industrial Revolution.

According to Martin Ford,[3] what is different this time is the speed of the advancements in a range of technologies collectively known as manufacturing 4.0, which includes robotics, 3D printing, autonomous vehicles, and so on.

AI is the use of data analysis and complex math to tease out useful insight from enormous amounts of data and to be able to do things as result of that insight. Innovations such as natural language recognition and simultaneous translation are also driven by AI technology.

One of the things that is driving the digital revolution is the enormous amount of data now available and the even larger amounts of data which is on its way as more and more devices and activities are connected to each other. The internet of things (IOT) is about adding the capability to store and transmit data to most objects through advanced sensors and electronics creating a web of information potentially connecting everything we interact with in our daily lives.

Digital density

One way of looking at the digital revolution is given by my colleagues Sandra Sieber and Evgeny Kaganer. The term they use is to look at the *digital density* of a given business or activity. Another way to see *digital density* is to think about how far has the digital revolution gone in that aspect of human activity.

The idea is to imagine what the impact on a specific business will be when digital density reaches 100 percent meaning that everything that can be digitized has been and that the full power of automation, connectivity and AI has come into play.

The music industry, for example, was one of the first to experience profound transformation due to the digitalization of music, and the repercussions of that are still playing out. You might say that its digital density is high.

Types of tasks

Oxford University's Carl Frey and Michael Osborne also looked digitalization's impact on different activities.[4] Their approach is to break down a specific

---

3 Martin Ford, *The Rise of the Robots: Technology and the Threat of a Jobless Future* (New York: Hachette Book Group, 2015).

4 C. Frey and M. Osborne, "The Future of Employment: How Susceptible Are Jobs to Computerisation?" Oxford Martin Programme on Technology and Employment (2013).

activity into its parts and then classify those parts. They talk about perception and manipulation, for example, by which they mean the ability to see things, touch them and move them around. This, they maintain, is different from creative intelligence or the ability to think up new things and social intelligence which has to do with understanding how other people will relate to them. Frey and Osborne then compare these ideas to figure out how much a task is worth or its overall value.

Machines have been getting better at perception and manipulation but still lag far behind people in many activities. Creative and social intelligence are areas where even the best algorithms have been unable to make too much progress in recent years. There is, in fact, a danger that expert systems and other algorithms will assume the bias that has been in the data they are using perpetuating racist and sexist policies over time.

Implications

Digitalization and automation were already transforming the world before the pandemic, and the pace of that transformation has accelerated. Robots and algorithms do not get sick and need no protection or health care benefits. With the imposition of travel restrictions, many of us learned how to do what we do online and from a distance.

As these changes spread across the economy, the impact will be tremendous. In the first place, digital technology has the potential to eliminate millions of jobs and also to change the way many others are carried out.

One scenario is that jobs will largely involve human interaction with robots and software systems in a collaborative way. Another is that all types of jobs and professions at the high end of the economic scale will enjoy more longevity as wealthier people will pay more money for a human touch.

While there are many voices expressing concern over the impact on people's livelihoods and the social fabric of society as a result of digitalization, others believe that we need automation to compensate for falling birth rates in the advanced economies.

In any case what is clear is that there will be a profound impact as the transformation makes its way from industry to industry in different parts of the world.

In another work, *The Technology Trap*, Carl Frey insists that these changes will be as dramatic as earlier technological improvements were to professions such as gas lighters, elevator operators and the people who once manned the telephone switchboards.

In his prescient book published in 2001, *The Future of Success*, Robert Reich believes that the best jobs would go to the people who will build the digital future and the product managers and marketing types who will figure out business models to make the new ideas economically viable.

Digitalization is also having an enormous impact on where you choose to live and work.

In his book, *Who's Your City?* Richard Florida describes a spikey world where wealth and innovation are increasingly concentrated in mega cities and hubs. In his research he has found that people in such places have more to do with others in similar situations, wherever they are located, than with people in other communities in their own countries.

Enrico Moretti goes deeper into the connection between the tech hubs and inequalities in *The New Geography of Jobs* and finds stark differences in wealth and even life expectancy between people living in the emerging tech hubs and others in communities which have been left behind. A point that both authors make is that life in the tech hubs is better for all of the residents regardless of whether their *roles* are directly related to new technology or if they fulfill other services such as working in the public or services sector.

These trends also play out at the political level in many countries around the world as it is clear that not everyone has benefited from globalization, digitalization and the knowledge economy in equal ways. Inequality leads to anger which leads to populist movements.

This inequality was particularly evident during the pandemic and associated lockdowns. People who do their work on computers and the telephone were largely able to stay home and continue to work. On the other hand, many people whose work requires their physical presence found themselves laid off or furloughed.

As the world continues on its digital journey, these differences may become even more severe and thus I urge you to consider how you will manage during the transformation.

The Natural Environment

The fourth and final issue I will discuss is the increasingly alarming situation concerning the environment. Air and water pollution have become critical issues in many parts of the world and especially in the mega cities of Asia, Latin America and Africa. The World Health Organization estimates that much of humanity lives in places with toxic air and contaminated water.

To a large degree, these problems, and the potentially larger issue of climate change, are the direct result of the increase in wealth and prosperity discussed earlier.

Interestingly enough, the pandemic has actually had a positive impact on the natural world. Many cities around the world, for example, have experienced sharp improvements in air quality during the shutdowns ordered to control the spread of the virus. Carbon emissions also went down 7 percent in 2020. In a similar way, the war in Ukrane is likely to accelerate Europe's transition to clean energy in order to reduce its reliance on Russian gas.

Climate change is a complex issue and is mainly related to the amount and type of energy we use. The good news is that wind and solar are now cheaper than fossil fuels in providing electricity and there is a broad-based movement of industries, cities and a number of countries around the world tend to move to a low carbon energy mix (see Box 1).

BOX 1: CLIMATE CHANGE

The idea that excessive amounts of carbon dioxide in the atmosphere were warming the earth was first documented by Charles Keeling in the early 1960s. At that time there was little-to-no awareness that modern industrial society could have an impact on the planet, although the dangerous effects of air and water pollution had become clear.

In 1968, an Astronaut on Apollo 8, Bill Anders, managed to photograph the earth rising over the lunar horizon. When it was published, the picture, called "Earthrise" changed humanity's perspective.

The first Earth Day was celebrated in 1970 and in 1972 the US Environmental Protection Agency was founded and the UN adopted the Stockholm Declaration which called for member states to protect the earth from the side effects of industrialization.

Twenty years later, the UN established the Framework Convention on Climate Change (UNFCCC) in Rio de Janeiro. The scientific background to the convention was prepared by the Intergovernmental Panel on Climate Change (IPCC) which had been created by the United Nations four years before that to build the world's scientific understanding of the issue.

These two entities, one political and the other scientific, have been the basis for finally reaching the Paris Agreement in 2015 after 21 meetings of the parties to the convention and the first four assessment reports published every five years or so by the IPCC.

The Paris agreement set the goal of keeping global warming between 1.5 and 2°C over pre-industrial times and each country agreed to meet their own voluntary targets or nationally determined contributions to that end. The idea is that over time these targets will be increased in the additional meetings such as the 2022 meeting in Cairo.

Part of the issue to balance the legitimate desire of the developing world to bring prosperity (and energy) to its populations with the need to do so in a sustainable way and the funding mechanism is designed to finance that development with money forms the more advanced economies.

Potable water is probably the most pressing issue in terms of resources around the world, although some analysts are concerned about specific minerals such as lithium and cobalt.

The United Nations estimates that two billion people live in countries undergoing extreme water stress and that double that amount experience water shortages at least one month during the year. Draught affects millions of people every year and has caused humanitarian crisis over time in Syria, Ethiopia and Yemen just to name a few of the countries affected.

Desalination is increasingly looked as the solution, but even with the latest Israeli technology, it takes enormous amount of energy to produce fresh water from the sea. That energy, in turn, needs to be produced in one way or another potentially adding to the overall problem.

Finally, the gradual warming of the planet itself is already having an impact on weather patterns and the climate in a number of places.

Implications

Environmental issues create both problems and opportunities for people as they think about what to do with their professional lives. Changes to the natural environment will, over time, limit the quality of life and prosperity of cities and regions and can have a negative impact on a number of industries and jobs at both the local and regional levels.

My conviction is that each one of us has the ability and even the responsibility to think about how this issue may impact us and our family. This will depend, of course, on where we live and work and also how we feel about the issue. In terms of looking ahead to your professional future, the natural environment may have an impact on the *place* you live, the *space* you work in and even the *role* you choose to play.

Perhaps the primary impact of environmental change will play out in the choices you make about where to live and work. In a number of specific parts of the world the situation is already alarming and has to do with draught and desertification, flooding, wild fires, pollution and stronger storms.

With regards to storms, the science is fairly straightforward. Slightly warmer temperatures in the sea and the atmosphere provide more energy for storms making them stronger. What makes the situation more dramatic is that we have steadily built up our communities along the world's coastlines. Natural resilience to storms is provided by wetlands which have been dried up to make way for development and much of the construction has not been sufficient to withstand the more powerful storms, storm surges and in some cases tsunamis.

This is part of the reason why storm damage, in terms of dollars, has increased in recent years but should be part of the calculation when looking at beach front property or communities that are highly vulnerable such as the greater Miami area.

A gradually warming earth will also impact other *places* changing land use patterns, crops and other aspects of life.

Environmental issues will also drive some business areas to rise and others to fall. In the first place, whole classes of industries are being targeted by governments and civil society for the local and global harm they are thought to do to the environment and jobs in these sectors may be at risk.

An industry which has been explicitly targeted is the coal business. Coal currently accounts for approximately 27 percent of the global energy mix but produces about 40 percent of carbon emissions. Substituting coal for natural gas in producing electrical power reduces emissions but between 50 and 60 percent and is one of the quickest ways to reduce emissions.

There are, on the other hand, tremendous opportunities connected to cleaning up the environment and making the transition to a low carbon economy. Christiana Figueres, who led the United Nations in its efforts to broker the Paris Agreement on climate change back in 2015, sees the transition as the biggest business opportunity of all time that will generate 65 million new jobs. Ms. Figueras and others have no doubt that the transition is coming, although the timing is not certain. Either the world will act in the next 10 years to address its ecological problems or it will be forced to do so by mother nature herself some years later.

Renewable energy and energy management show enormous potential as do a host of well-established technologies in the area of energy efficiency that can be done by carpenters, plumbers and electricians.

Concerns about air pollution have led cities around the world to ban diesel engines as of 2030, and most major car manufacturers are already phasing out diesel and developing electric cars and light trucks.

Other opportunities have to do with managing the likely effects of climate change. A former student of mine, for example, runs a company dedicated to increasing the resilience of port facilities around the world. He tells me that business is booming as his clients prepare for slightly higher water levels and significantly higher storm surge from hurricanes and typhoons.

Extreme weather events as well as the slow effects of climate change will also have a huge impact on a wide range of business areas from construction to food production.

Finally, the challenges associated with the environment are creating new classes of jobs. A new segment of the auditing industry, for example, has emerged to help companies track their performance and publish their sustainability reports.

There are also new jobs associated with new forms of energy such as the people who build, operate and service wind farms and solar power facilities.

One of the pillars of Joe Biden's economic program is to accelerate the transition to a low carbon economy, and his administration believes that there will be millions of good jobs available as the United States rebuilds its aging infrastructure and makes buildings across the country more energy efficient.

The last aspect of the issue on how the environment affects each one of us is more about our own attitudes and concerns on the issue. Millions of people are taking active steps to avoid or eliminate single-use plastic from their daily lives, reuse clothing and other durable products and participate in the circular economy in one way or another.

Everything Is Connected

Before closing this chapter on trends, I just want to make the point that these trends are connected with each other and other issues that I have not discussed here in order to save space.

Other issues include the shortage of key resources such as water and specific minerals needed to build an electronic and sustainable future, political trends within countries, income inequality and a host of other social issues.

Globalization and digitalization, for example, contribute to income inequality which drives migration. Lower incomes and immigration then feeds
frustration in some developed countries which in turn leads to populist politics.

Coming back to the issue of career planning, my conviction is that each
one of should have some idea of where these and other trends might take them.

Key Ideas Chapter 1

- The world is changing quickly, and it is essential that you develop your
  own view as to which trends will impact you, your family and the work
  you do.
- The evolution of health care and the related issue of its cost and access is
  likely to be one of these trends.
- The world is in a complex moment in terms of geopolitics, and the war in
  Ukraine which began in March 2022 is just one example of a number of
  conflicts.
- Digital technology has taken a giant step forward as a result of the pandemic, yet, the massive introduction of these technologies brings dangers
  as well as benefits.
- Climate change and the degradation of our natural environment are the
  direct results of the increasing wealth and prosperity of an increasing
  large global population.
- These trends are connected and affect each other in complex ways.

CHAPTER 2

SETTING A COURSE

Whether the pandemic and the current war has caused you to stop and think or you have lost your job to the general reshuffling on the economy that is underway, you may be asking yourself in which direction to take your professional life.

If this is the case, the most important question is, what do you want to do?

You may not have an answer to this question and perhaps that is what drew you to *Learning to Fly* in the first place. Maybe you have been wrestling with the issue for months or perhaps have never really thought about it.

Some people answer the question in a way which is genuine but not useful in terms of job hunting. They will typically talk about wanting to work with people, make an impact or find a better work–life balance. Other answers have to do with finding the right kind of environment such as a small or large company with a certain kind of culture or style.

Maybe you have only figured out what you don't want to do which is at least a good start.

The most common response I get from men and women in their late 20s and early 30s is that they are open to "many things or even anything." This might be what you are thinking, but, in my experience, it is probably not true and in any case is not really good enough.

Experienced people often respond to the question in terms of what they have been doing so far. They tell me they "know about this or that and have experience in a specific part of the economy." What they often do not say is what they really want.

While it does not have to be too specific, it is critically important to set a course so that you can at least point yourself in the right direction. Without it, you will literally be adrift in the sea of life.

You Have to Choose

My conviction is that it is far better to make a choice and focus your energies on a specific direction that has to do with what you really want as opposed to keeping your options open or staying with what you already know. This is especially true in the current environment when conviction and a sense of purpose are essential to getting a good job.

I understand the instinct to keep your options open. The essential logic is that by not choosing you can increase your chances of finding gainful employment. This is a widely held belief, but it is wrong for seven reasons:

The first reason why you need to make some choice is that there are too many options and paths available. When thinking about what to do, many people seem like a kid in a candy store with a few dollars for the first time. The choice can be overwhelming and quite stressful since virtually any subject branches off into a number of directions.

The danger of looking at too many things is that you may be overwhelmed by the number of choices and do nothing, or perhaps take the first opportunity which comes along regardless of whether it is the "right" one.

The second reason is that you will need help along the way, and it will be difficult for people to help you if you do not know what you want. In Lewis Carroll's *Alice's Adventures in Wonderland*, the Cheshire cat answers Alice's question about which way to go by saying "that depends a good deal on where you want to get to." Knowing what you want to do will earn the respect of others who may then choose to go out of their way to help you along the path.

The third reason is that nobody wants to hire anybody who does not have a convincing and burning interest in the job in question. My first job after university was in the oil drilling business, and I once asked the man who hired me why he picked me over the other students who had applied. His answer was simply that "you wanted the job," and ever since then I have seen this play out again and again.

People like to hire people who are motivated, interested and even passionate about whatever is the essential nature of the position. This is true regardless of whether that has to with developing advanced technology, building market share for a specific product, crunching numbers or saving the planet. True interest is hard to fake, and these days such authentic connection is more important than ever.

The fourth reason that focus rather than keeping one's options open is important is that it will help you avoid dividing your efforts among different directions. Time, contacts and energy are all finite resources, and in my experience it is a bad idea to spread them too thin.

Good homework is very time-consuming, and you will not do a good job in researching a specific company, market or sector if you are not focused. You demonstrate your interest by doing your homework, and it is easy to see the difference between someone who has taken the time to do their research and someone who has not.

The fifth reason to choose has to do with your responsibility to others. There are people who are genuinely open to different types of work, different industries and living in different places. While some might call such people free spirited or adventurous, I find it to be somewhat irresponsible depending on where you are in your life.

If you have already started a family, for example, then it makes sense to think about the medium-term and long-term prospects of a given path. Even before that or after the kids have gone off to pursue their own paths, we all have some responsibilities to others and may want to think about the impact our choices have on them.

The sixth reason to choose is that commitment can be a powerful tool, and it only works when it is real. I have found this to be true as clarity of purpose focuses a person's efforts and, most importantly, improves their probability of being successful through what Deepak Chopra refers to as synchronicity. For Chopra, clarity of purpose or intention can help us be open to possibilities that we may not otherwise see (see Box 2).

BOX 2: INTENTION

Have you ever found a parking place exactly where you needed it or had all the lights turn green as if by magic? Deepak Chopra is an author who explores the intersection between modern science, medicine and Hindu spirituality. One of his books, Synchro Destiny,[1] introduces an idea he calls synchronicity. My own understanding of the concept is that we can, to some degree, control our own destiny through developing and using our intention.

Chopra maintains that there are no coincidences. In his view, things are always lining up to make our dreams possible but that we may not be paying sufficient attention to our surroundings and are thus unable to spot the thousands of opportunities that cross our paths. His view is that when our intention is pure and our mind is open to such possibilities, they manifest themselves in the world.

---

1 D. Chopra, *Synchro Destiny* (London: Ebury Press, 2005).

I have found this to be true in my work with people who are clear about their professional goals.

In its 2003 film, *Finding Nemo*, Pixar studios and Director Andrew Stanton tell the story of Marlin, a small and timid clown fish who sets off to find his missing son Nemo who has been taken by a scuba diving dentist to his office in Australia.

In Spanish, the film was called *Buscando a Nemo*, meaning "Looking for Nemo." There is a world of difference between *finding* Nemo and *looking for* him. This is the essence of synchronicity.

Are you "looking for a job" or "finding your path"? There is a difference.

Clarity of purpose will allow you to talk to different people about what you are planning to do. They will in turn respect your conviction and some will do their best to try to help.

In the end they may know someone who can help you directly or even hire you right away for a short-term project in your area of interest. That may then lead to your attending a meeting or a conference where you meet someone else who has been looking for someone just like you for a permanent position.

Coincidence? Hard work? Magic or all of the above?

The seventh and final reason to choose is that if you don't know what you're looking for it seems to me that you may never find it. The pursuit of happiness will be discussed further in Chapter 7 and the larger issue of purpose in Chapter 11. Nevertheless, what we do with our professional life is an important part of how we spend our time and perhaps who we are or will come to be and deserves some careful thought.

How to Choose?

To help you with the question about what you want to do, I suggest a framework which has helped thousands of people over the years. The framework is shown in Figure 2.1 and combines your past experience, the constraints or limitations which affect you and what you are really passionate about.

I have found the framework useful in the past but feel it is even more important today because digitalization has made it easier for potential employers to

FIGURE 2.1   Framework.

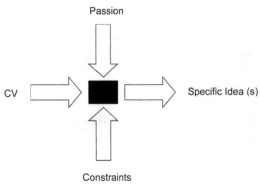

meet more people and, at the same time, harder for you, or anyone else, to break through and be heard. For that to happen you have to have very clear ideas that you can explain and defend even if you are on a zoom link.

Essentially the idea is to look deeply into the three different concepts and use them to choose a few concrete options about what to do.

Past experience has to do with what you have actually done. Where do you come from? What languages do you speak and with which cultures are you familiar?

Constraints have to do with family commitments, money requirements and other personal issues which will limit your choices if you are honest with yourself.

Passion is what really makes you excited. It might be a product, a service, a way of interacting with others. It might be a specific sport or type of travel. In my experience everyone is passionate about something, and the challenge is often to actually articulate what that really is.

The black box in the middle of Figure 2.1 represents the step that very few people actually take. It has to do with solving the equation for yourself. What actual job might exist in the world where a potential employer will value your experience; where you will be able to fulfill your commitments to your friends, family and banker and where you will actually have a chance to do something for which you can be passionate about?

This step is both analytical and creative in that it forces you to think through the issues involved and dream up a story which makes sense.

Past Experience

You are who you are. You grew up in one or several places, speak certain languages, went to certain schools and have worked in a series of jobs. You cannot change the past.

What you can do is to write your curriculum vitae (CV) or resume in different ways to stress different aspects of your background or experience, but before we get to that, the first step is to take an honest look at your experience and tease out what it is that makes up who you are in terms of your professional profile.

Sectors

Whether you are just starting your career or an experienced manager in their 40s, 50s or 60s, you will have some experience in certain parts of the economy and less in others. Is it in automotive, aerospace or travel and tourism?

Drilling down further in the hotel business, for example, there is the front office, food and beverage, housekeeping, security, and so on. At the corporate level there are also IT and human resource (HR) managers, property development people and mergers and acquisition at the highest level.

A related question is which companies did you work in as there will be differences in approach and corporate culture. This might be related to the company targeting the high end or the value segment of a specific market or the location of head office and where members of the management team are from.

Countries, regions and languages

Where have you lived? Have you traveled widely or perhaps studied in another city or even another country?

Did you grow up in the same place or move around like I did? Did you, perhaps, spend some of your formative years in another country as do many children of diplomats, military personnel and corporate managers and executives.

On a broader level, which cultures do you feel some affinity for or have some understanding of?

While my own childhood was spent in the suburbs of New York and Boston, my son-in-law's father was a diplomat, and he grew up in different countries including Mozambique and Morocco. He not only speaks five or six languages fluently but even more importantly has some cultural affinity for Europe and Africa as well as for what it's like to live in an Islamic society.

Even within the United States there are important cultural differences between different regions of the country and in some places, such as Miami, many people speak Spanish.

Skills

Skills go beyond titles or job descriptions to get at what you know how to do. This can have a wide variety of answers such as marketing consumer products to low-income people or managing complex IT projects. The more specific, the better, and it is also important to identify what you are best at as well as what you do not do so well.

Diving deeply into your skill set can also take you into the realization that your true calling may lie in so-called soft skills such as client management or even less obvious traits such as attention to detail or empathic ability.

Style

I find that leadership style is also important as there are some people who fit well into specific industries or roles and others who will always struggle. There are literally thousands of books available on leadership style, and it almost does not matter what terminology or framework you use.

Probably the most famous one was developed by Katharine Briggs and her daughter Isabel Briggs Myers during the 1940s and 1950s and is largely based on the work of Carl Jung. Whatever you use, the key thing is to be aware of how you interact with other people.

Not everyone can be the captain or the quarterback, and the most important idea is to know ourselves as well as we can.

Crucible moments

The last idea in this list of taking inventory is the idea of crucible moments[2] developed by Warren Bennis and Robert Thomson. In interviewing a number of successful business leaders, they found that many could articulate specific influential moments that were "a trial and a test, a point of deep self-reflection that forced them to question who they were and what mattered to them."

---

2   W. Bennis and R. Thomas, "Crucibles of Leadership." *Harvard Business Review*, September 2002.

Have you experienced such moments in your own professional or personal life? How did you manage during the sharp economic downturn of 2009 or some other important crisis. More recently, how did you get through the pandemic and the economic hardship that the containment measures implemented in many countries caused? Looking at such moments might add additional insight into who you are and what you can do.

Chapter 3 will discuss how to put these elements together into a coherent story, but before that, it is important just to be clear with yourself what you have done, know how to do and what parts of the world you are familiar with.

Money and Other Constraints

Constraints are the things that limit what we can choose to do. They are about what's important and necessary in life.

In my experience, the most critical constraints that need to be considered are money, work–life balance, geographic limits and ethical redlines. While you might have others, the important thing is to make them explicit to yourself.

Money

Financial or economic issues are important and anyone looking for a job or a career change ought to carefully think through their financial needs. For me, the key point here is how much do you need, not how much do you want, or what you can get.

I put the emphasis on needs because I do not think that money should be the prime motivation for choosing what to do, although it is important to have enough. I have found that many people think about financial rewards as a scorekeeping system which allows them to keep track of how well they are doing relative to their past and peers. This is a mistake.

If, instead, you look at what you really need, you can come up with very different career options which still keep food on the table but also allow you to develop new skills or pursue something you are truly passionate about. In my own life I took a very substantial pay cut when I left the business world for a job in academia and have never regretted the move.

Work–life balance

In addition to looking at your professional options, I urge you to consider the people around you and your shared future.

When I was growing up my father would change jobs every three to five years and usually our family would follow him at the end of the school year. He traveled constantly, and it was a rare event if he was home for dinner on a weeknight. There was a time in my life when I also had a very demanding travel schedule and now know how hard that was for my family.

Some jobs require a certain kind of lifestyle or commitment, and it is important to know what is important before you even consider them.

I know many people who found that measures implemented to contain the pandemic gave them an unexpected opportunity to stop traveling or working late at the office and to connect with their families.

What is important is to include the kind of balance you seek between your professional and personal life in the process of thinking through what to do. The key is to make trade-offs clear to yourself and the people around you.

Mobility

At my school we run some training programs for the United Nations. On those courses I have met amazing men and women who live and work in very difficult places but do so because they believe that their work is so important that it justifies the risks and hardships.

Millions of Ukranians have, of course, left their country as a result of the invasion seeking safety from Russian bombs and rockets.

Location can also be a constraint if you already have a life partner or children, are in a serious relationship or simply do not want to be too far away from your wider family and friends.

Your partner might have their own career goals and limitations. A former colleague on the faculty is married to woman who is a member of the Italian Parliament. After commuting for a couple of years he finally moved to Italy so he could be with her and their children.

The final issue having to do with family is that people in their 40s and 50s are increasingly taking on responsibilities for aging parents. As we and our parents live longer, this constraint will become increasingly important.

What can you live with?

The last constraint I want to call attention to are the ethical dimensions connected to specific roles or jobs in a number of sectors and places.

In the first place, there are corrupt practices in many industries and in many parts of the world. Certainly, the legal framework in some countries is very different than in others, and what might be normal business to some people could be thought of as crime by others.

The purpose of bringing this up is not to go into depth on business ethics but to stress the idea that certain behaviors are normal in certain positions and if you are uncomfortable with or unwilling to engage in them then my advice is to not take a job in that industry or company!

A second set of constraints might come up in connection with certain activities that you do not want to be associated with. Beyond the obvious category of illegal activities, you may feel strongly about fossil fuels, tobacco or something else.

A very recent example are Russian professionals who have left Russia since they do not want to support its actions in Ukraine. The important idea is to be aware of any red lines that you are unwilling to cross.

Passion

I started speaking with executives who were looking for work and with students about *passion* because I found that many would articulate what they wanted to do with little-to-no energy and would struggle to connect to something more authentic.

Instead of talking about what they are really passionate about, people answer my question with ideas which might be true but are neither compelling nor particularly helpful. They say they want to "work with people," "be in an international, creative environment" or something along those lines. The problem is it's very hard to help someone with such vague interests.

One of the things that has always intrigued me is how there is a complex web of companies behind every facet of the world we live in, and with a little thought, creativity and homework one can begin to drill down into virtually anything.

If you have a passion for toy soldiers, kite surfing or bubble bath, there is an industrial ecosystem which is manufacturing these items and a complex supply chain going both upstream to raw material manufacturers and downstream to distributors and retailers as well as in many cases service providers, specialty websites, and so on.

In my case, while my first passion has always been for boats, I did spend a lot of time in the automotive industry, and I do not think I would have been able to do so without a genuine interest in cars and trucks. My attitude is that if you are going to spend 60–80 hours a week dealing with a business, then it is extremely helpful to have some fundamental identification with the product or service that is offered.

The most important thing is that in the absence of experience or qualifications, passion is often the only thing that one has to convince a potential employer to give you a chance! If your passion burns bright enough, it is sometimes enough.

The hard part, for many people, is to actually look inside themselves deeply enough to be able to identify what their passion really is! Some people have known all their life and can tell you straight away. Others, it seems don't know or don't remember.

What is your passion?

If it's hard for you to articulate what you are passionate about, I suggest you try to remember what you wanted to be when you were 6 or 16? Did you have a clear idea at one point in your life? What happened to that? Did you want to be a doctor, an astronaut, a fireman, a fashion designer?

While it might be too late for you to follow such dreams, you can still leverage that interest into a meaningful career path. If, as a child, you played with fire trucks, then as an adult you might be able to make your living selling or servicing them!

In another example, while most of us would never qualify for astronaut training, there is a, fast-growing, space industry which needs all types of skills from engineers to financial controllers, HR managers and operations experts.

If you do not remember what you wanted to be, ask your aunt or uncle, as they will. I do not recommend asking your parents because it might cause them some concern if their 30-, 40- or 50-year-old daughter or son is rethinking their career. A favorite aunt, on the other hand, will happily explain whatever your interest was back in the day.

There are two dangers in working with what you are truly passionate about. One is that you might lose yourself in the subject matter and become a one-dimensional, workaholic. The other is that by getting involved in the business end of something you might lose part of the romance of the thing. I prefer, for example, sailing for pleasure rather than working in the marine industry.

While I agree that you may not want to work in the area that you are most passionate about, I do feel strongly that you should not seek out a product or service area for which you have no feeling whatsoever.

In my view one of the biggest benefits of being clear about your passion is that it makes it much more likely for you to get help along the way. Not only will a perspective employer be impressed by your genuine interest but others will also.

Senior managers are generally looking for talent all the time. It's actually quite difficult to find people with true interest and high level of energy, and when a friend or acquaintance sends one to you, the normal response is gratitude.

Once you have a clear idea of who you are, what constraints you have and what you really care about, then the next step is to think through different possibilities using the three dimensions discussed above.

Your Own Case Study

My advice is to write your own case study. Answer the question about what to do based on your experience, constraints and passion. Putting these three ideas together allow for a structured and creative process of figuring out in which *space*, or field of endeavor, you should seek to work, the *role* you would like to play and the *place* meaning the region or city in you hope to live. These three dimensions are discussed at length in chapters 4, 5 and 6.

It is probably a good idea to start with one of the three dimensions and then seek out the other two.

Some people will be looking for a job in Barcelona or Boston, and my advice to them is to then look honestly at the industrial fabric of the city and pick an industry or a *space* in which they have or can develop a true interest. In terms of function or *role*, probably they should look for a way to do something similar to what they have done before or that at least uses some of the same skills.

Others will be excited to get into a specific *space* such as alternative energy or fashion or investment banking.

In this case, then the next question in my view should be in which *role* can you add the most value. The last point will be location or *place* and the question is to either go to the center of the industry (e.g., New York City for fashion and banking) or make a conscious choice to go to a place where the industry is smaller and possibly less competitive.

Finally, some people will choose the *role* they want to play first and then think about everything else afterward. In this case, I think it is sensible to look at those *spaces* in which that *role* itself is key in that business. Marketing, for example, is typically what drives consumer goods companies.

This analysis, for example, led a lawyer I know to reexamine his career working on the legal team of one of the largest hospital groups in the United States. As a boy his passion had been sports, but he followed his family's advice and went to law school after college.

Fast forward 15 years and he was living a relatively expensive lifestyle with a young family and making very good money for a job he did not enjoy in an industry for which he had no passion.

The challenge was to reconnect with his true passion but do so in a way which could maintain his family's lifestyle and stay in the same city since his wife's career was taking off. In other words, he had to determine the *space* in which to work, the *role* to play and the *place* in which to work and live.

Part of the answer to the lawyer's dilemma lay in looking deeper at his experience and understanding that his true gift was developing meaningful client relationships and that his detailed knowledge of labor law could be an added benefit in the field of executive recruitment. He is currently director of a large firm's sports industry practice, and the thinking he did is summarized in Figure 2.2.

Interestingly enough, after changing *space* and *role*, the lawyer was able to change the place he and his family live. As a result of the pandemic, his company moved all of its activities online, and most of his colleagues actually left New York City on a temporary basis. In this environment, he realized that it no longer mattered where he lived and therefore decided to move to Tel-Aviv!

What is key is for each one of us to develop a clear idea of one or two combinations of *space*, *role* and *place* that we will be able to be passionate about, live within our constraints and for which some aspect of our experience will be useful.

FIGURE 2.2   Framework applied to a lawyer.

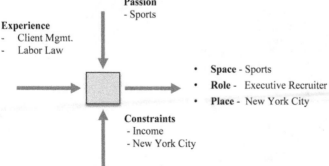

Passion
- Sports

Experience
- Client Mgmt.
- Labor Law

- **Space** - Sports
- **Role** - Executive Recruiter
- **Place** - New York City

Constraints
- Income
- New York City

Ideally, the combinations you come up with will make sense in terms of your overall trajectory. The best way to do this is to look at your own career path up until today and learn to tell your own story in a compelling way. If you get it right, your story will help you discover an exciting combination and also explain why it makes sense for you.

Chapter 3 focuses on telling your story, and then after that chapters 4, 5, and 6 explore the different elements of the framework.

Key Ideas Chapter 2

- The most important question is what do you want to do?
- You should come up with a clear answer to that question for seven reasons.
  1. There are too many options;
  2. It's hard to help someone who does not know what they want;
  3. True interest is hard to fake;
  4. Good homework is key and takes a lot of time;
  5. Commitment brings serendipity which can have results;
  6. If others depend on you it is your responsibility to choose wisely;
  7. You will be happier if you seek out what you want.
- Before thinking about what's next, it is very important to reflect on your past experience, the constraints you face and the things you are or could be truly passionate about.
- A choice about what to do involves selecting a *space*, or field of endeavor, a *role* to play in that *space* and a *place* in which to live and work.

CHAPTER 3

TELLING YOUR STORY

In the context of looking for work, almost any casual chat, initial meeting or formal job interview will start with the question *What Are You Doing Now?* Since March 2020, the answer for many people has been *not very much* because of the pandemic and its economic fallout.

This question is connected to a broader one which is sometimes asked directly and sometimes implied by the first question and is *What Is Your Story?* The broader story question is really an invitation to explain who you are and how the other person should engage with you.

In my role as a headhunter and later in the business school I would often start with the second question to get a sense of who I was talking to. Some people's stories are full of anger or a deep sense of betrayal as they have lost their job and feel they have been treated poorly or unfairly. Other stories are more upbeat and give a sense of possibility and future potential. Some are fascinating, while others are predictable or a bit confusing.

What many people's story show is how little conscious thought they had apparently put into choosing the overall direction of their professional life. A deeper issue is that many people really do not seem to know how they have got to where they are.

You may find that by working on your own story you also may help yourself see what the next chapter of that story ought to be.

Your future choices are, in part, determined by what you have done in the past and an honest and objective accounting of how you have arrived at a specific point in your professional lives is the first step into looking ahead and thinking about what to do.

Because digging through our past choices can be difficult, I use two metaphors for the purpose.

When I have used the metaphors in lectures and one-on-one meetings, I have found that different people usually identify more with one or the other but seldom both. If one of them rings true to you, it may help you craft the best version of your own story.

After discussing the two metaphors this chapter will get into the mechanics of how to craft your story and cover your past, present and future. It will finally show you how to look into the future and start crafting the next chapters in your story.

The River

The first metaphor compares our professional development to traveling down a river in a raft or canoe. When traveling down a river, it is the river itself that determines the direction and speed that you are able to go. This metaphor might strike you if you do not currently feel a strong connection for the way you earn a living.

Rivers can be compared metaphorically to sectors, industries or the idea of *spaces* that I will discuss in more depth in Chapter 4. The comparison has a number of different aspects.

The starting point

Maybe you started your professional trajectory some years ago by answering an advertisement or doing an internship. Perhaps a member of your family or a teacher made an introduction for you.

If you are like many people, you took your first job with little or no thought about where it would eventually lead to. Maybe you thought to yourself that the job was only going to be for the summer or until something else would happen. Maybe you were just thrilled to be actually making money and did not think too much about the future. Something like this typically happens in our late teens or early 20s when we are still thinking about who we are and our ideas about what to do are still incomplete.

In terms of the river, we start our trip by putting our boat in the water in whatever river happens to be closest or most accessible to us.

Progress and direction

As time goes by your internship might have turned into a job and that job then might lead to a promotion in the same organization. Later, your old boss or a headhunter might have recruited you to another company in the same field. If you think about your professional life in these terms, you might see that you may have just went along with the current, perhaps jumping into a different boat from time to time.

In nature, rivers sometimes change their course or even dry up. For many people in the hospitality and tourism business, spring and summer of 2020 were the worst they had ever seen. Even without a global pandemic, rivers can dry up because of a recession or changes in technology or consumer behavior.

For some, the solution has been to wait until the rains come back and the river start to flow. I have friends in the tourism business who have managed to hold on through the aslt two years and are finally seeing a recovery: will happen sooner rather than later.

Portage

Many people have decided to make a sharp change in their career path, and this might be your case. To stick with the idea of the river, this means changing to a different one.

A river will always take you in its own direction and at its own pace. In real life what this means is that if you have a personal goal which is different than that which the river is taking you, then you may have to find a different river all together. In long-distance canoeing, changing rivers is called portage and involves picking the boat up and carrying it over the mountains to another river.

Portage, or changing your trajectory, can be difficult as the trip itself may involve weeks or even months with the financial and psychological strain that goes with that process. You may even have to pick up your metaphorical boat and take it to another region or country as result of economic, political or geopolitical changes.

A student of mine in her early 40s made the point that the longer you wait to change, the heavier your boat gets as you load it up with spouses, children, property and other commitments.

Slower and faster

Many years ago I was on a rafting trip in water that was so slow that I gave up after an hour and paddled back to the starting place. The heat and mosquitos were driving me crazy, and I felt we were making no progress.

Many of our full-time MBA students come on the program because they feel they are going nowhere in their current jobs or at least not moving fast enough or having enough of an impact. Other people come to me thinking of quitting their current job because they feel they are learning very little and moving much too slowly.

A river might also have moments of great intensity as the water speeds up and runs through the rapids. Rapids are categorized from 1 to 5, and amateurs like myself are not encouraged to go past category 3 without expert guides and training.

I have found moments in my professional life that have been the equivalent of category 4 or 5 rapids. At those times I felt that I needed to focus all of my energies on keeping the boat upright and getting through the next project or position.

The danger is that when dealing with such situations many of us lose track of the things that are more important like our spouses, family, friends and even our health. Perhaps the biggest danger at such times is that it can be difficult to see what is going on.

In my own case I thought it was normal to be away from home three to four nights a week and work all the time. If I had thought through the implications of spending so many years in the rapids on my most important relationships and health I would have made a different choice.

Capsizing

Another aspect of the metaphor is that it is very possible to fall out of a boat or capsize in a river. If you are lucky a colleague will help you to get back in the boat or pick you up somewhere downstream. In real life there are times when we lose our job, get fired or laid off, or realize that the only way to balance work and family or protect our health is to quit.

For many people the pandemic was the equivalent of an enormous wave that upset many boats and left them floundering in the water or washed up on the river bank.

Perhaps the most common mistake I see from people who have lost their job is to jump into the first boat they can in the same river without taking a bit of time to catch their breath on the shore and reconfirm that the river is in fact the right one for them.

If this is your situation then I would urge you to think about the river you have been on and be clear in your own head if it is really where you want to be. If it is then clearly look for a solid boat and get back on the water. If it is not, then this may be a good time to consider changing to something else.

Looking ahead

The last aspect of the metaphor is that if you want to know what the future might look like, then you may want to talk with people who are 10 or 20 years further down river than you are. They will be able to tell you if there have been rapids or periods of calm and what the river looks like far ahead.

One of the reasons I joined the faculty of the business school is that I did not see anyone in the consulting world who was where I wanted to be. While the best ones had been financially successful and seemed to enjoy their lives, I could not see myself as being satisfied in their shoes. There were several professors, on the other hand, who were 15–20 years older and seemed to have found a wonderful balance in their professional and personal life.

Does this metaphor strike you as helpful? Does it seem that your professional journey is, in some way, out of your own control and that you have been traveling down river for some time? If the answer to this question is yes then the deeper question is if you are in fact on the right river and going in the right direction?

The Race

The second metaphor compares our professional lives to an adventure race since advancement in many professions does feel a bit like a race against others, as well as ourselves, which plays out over different stages over the course of time.

The field

The race begins on a perfectly flat and well-maintained *field* which stretches out as far the eye can see. At this stage, the faster you run, the farther you get.

In my first job after the MBA, I was working in Madrid for an international consulting company and the office was led by a charismatic and demanding man. We would normally work till 8:00 or 9:00 p.m. and would often spend the week in another city on a project. The dark side of this pace would become evident as some of us started gaining weight, had problems with his or her relationship, and so on.

In the different multinationals, consultancies and financial services companies where my classmates and I worked, there was a clear link between the pace that each one was "running" and the immediate rewards in terms of bonuses and promotions.

The other thing which was apparent was that some people simply had to run faster than others who had for a number of reasons got a head start. A friend at that time started out working on an assembly line and put himself through engineering school at night. Later, he did an executive MBA and was promoted as principal when he was in his late 30s. He started further back than I did but simply worked harder and ran faster to catch up.

Other people get across the *field* very quickly with less effort because they are either smarter, more creative or luckier than most of the others around them.

The Rough

The next stage starts at the edge of the *field* where the gardeners no longer reach. Once you get into the *rough* the land becomes more uneven and rocky. Shrubs and bushes grow in unlikely places and small animals burrow little holes in the ground.

If you keep running as fast as you can in the *rough* and look straight ahead, you are likely to trip and fall. In business this has to do with setting a reasonable pace and avoiding pitfalls.

Support staff, for example, need to be treated with respect, and time has to be taken to get to know them and win their trust. You are expected to show up at company functions, dinner meetings, and so on, and need to remember not to drink too much or talk out of turn.

Another major pitfall is that men and women in the late 20s and early 30s tend to believe they can do everything and often do not allocate enough time to the tasks at hand.

When running across the *rough*, it is necessary to watch the ground and make small jumps to clear shrubs or dart around obstacles. The good news is that if you do fall and get hurt, you may find that someone helps you get back on your feet.

I remember one occasion after returning to the United States, when a Sr. Partner took me aside and let me know very clearly that I had come over as arrogant during a planning meeting. His tough feedback allowed me to change my behavior and get back on track.

The forest

After a time, the race will take you to a *forest*. At the edge of the *forest*, the danger is running full speed into a tree. I know many people who appear to have done just that in a professional sense. These were talented people who worked hard but were metaphorically watching the ground and did not see the tree until it was too late.

Examples of running into trees are about when you let your ego get in the way, are impatient or fail to see important social relationships between others. The result is a damaged reputation, missed opportunities or even the loss of the job. The challenge after one of these events is to pick yourself up, recognize what has happened and get moving again.

Confronted with the *forest* or after running into a tree or two, some people simply stop and remain at a certain level with their organization or profession. They will normally tell you that they don't like politics but sometimes there are deeper issues at play (see Box 3).

BOX 3: FORM AND SUBSTANCE

Over the years I have met many professional people who I would characterize as having not managed to make it through the forest for one reason or another. Some had clearly made a choice at one stage in their career to stress their technical rather than their managerial skill and have made their own peace with that decision.

Others have had the choice made for them due to one or a series of mishaps that have happened on the way. Such people, in my experience, never really understood that you can no longer run in the forest. They simply do not see the political pitfalls or pay attention to what is going beneath the surface.

There is, however, a third type of amazingly capable people who damage their prospects due to a mistaken understanding of the role of presence and politics in business life.

When I was in my early 30s a senior partner pulled me aside and told me I needed to dress better. I was astounded at the time but have come to understand what he meant.

One way of looking at professionals is to rank them along two dimensions being form and substance. Form is how good does a person look, how well do they talk, and to what degree are they sensitive to the people around them. Substance has to do with their technical skill, creativity, and ability to work hard.

Typically, people who have neither form nor substance do not make it very far in business.

I have known a number of people who are so strong in form that they have been able to compensate for an almost complete lack of substance and have done very well professionally.

Another type of person is the one who is strong on substance but very weak on form. This goes beyond the clothes they wear to the image they project and the way they present themselves and their own abilities.

As a professor I was puzzled why such talented people, many of whom are engineers, would not speak out more frequently in class and cultivate a stronger profile. The conclusion that I finally came to is that high-substance people often pull back from developing their own abilities in the area of form so that they would never appear to belong in the other category!

The thing is that you need to cultivate both form and substance to really make things happen.

Understanding the political realities of a situation and using that understanding is key to making things happen in any organization. Political awareness and abilities are one of the most valuable skills a manager can have and their lack is blatantly obvious in some cases.

The *forest* will get denser until it is reminiscent of the woods in *The Lord of the Rings* or *Harry Potter*. What's important is knowing where you are, staying on the path and having the skills needed to get through the *forest* in one piece.

The swamp

After the *forest*, comes the swamp. In the *swamp*, visibility is poor. The ground is damp, and your feet can sink into the ooze if you're not careful. There are, however, narrow paths through the swamp, but they require your full attention as the way ahead is often unclear.

It is also hard to predict where a path ends when you take it. It might start out going north but then twist around and appear to be heading east until it twists again toward the south!

Sometimes the path actually brings you to a dead end from which there is no way forward or you find yourself in a situation you did not want to be in terms of travel schedule, stress or work–life balance. A related point is that if a path takes you in the wrong direction, arriving sooner or later will not make things better.

A friend found himself taking on increasing responsibility as the CFO of a large company until one day his wife presented him with an ultimatum. Fortunately for their life together he left that position and then went on to raise money for start-ups.

If you realize that the path is heading the wrong way, there really is no choice but to retrace your steps back to the *forest* (if you can) and start again down another path!

The good news is that some of what you learned along the way might be useful as there are similarities in all industries and types of organizations. In my case, some of the skills I learned in management consulting helped me when I became a headhunter, and some of those skills help me in academia. In each instance, however, I did have to start a few steps back and start close to the beginning.

The beach

For me, the goal is a house overlooking the sea with a wide verandah from which I will be able to watch the boats go by and maybe go scuba diving once in a while. Other people go sailing, surfing or fishing. For some people it's all about the size and stature of the house, while others are happy with a small apartment or even a caravan.

My mother officially retired from the city she worked for almost 30 years ago and moved to a small house in a small town she had lived in before. Although she is officially retired, she is very busy and until very recently kept a part-time job in addition to her volunteer work and art classes.

Do you feel that you are somewhere in the race? Are you just starting out, in the *rough* or perhaps deep in the *forest* or the *swamp*? Perhaps the most important idea is to realize that different phases require different skills and a different pace.

For many people, Covid or the latest war have acted like earthquakes that shook the entire course, knocking down many of the people on it. If this is part of your story then the question is where were you when the earthquake happened? Some of you may be able to pick up wherever you left off, but others may need to go back a bit and start again.

Crafting the Story

Storytelling is an art, and some of us are better at it than others. There are, however, some basic ideas that will make your personal story as effective as it can be.

The first idea is that your story has to be true. Men and women who hire other people, or the HR specialists and headhunters who often get involved in the hiring process, have an ear for anything that does not ring true. They may not know which part of the story is exaggerated, misleading or an outright lie, but if they sense that something is false your candidacy will be rejected. It's that simple.

The second idea is that your story needs to be interesting and relatively brief. I suggest having a very short, elevator pitch and a longer one which might be told over a cup of coffee. The first one should be about two minutes, and the other one might take eight or ten. Both need to say the same thing with the difference being the level of detail.

If you have done many things in your life you may have to group them together into phases to make a punchier and more coherent narrative. I was, for example, a strategy consultant in two different firms, worked in several different countries and managed projects in a few different industries and over many different topics.

At this stage in my life, however, those 15 years can be collapsed to a very brief description which explains that since I was not sure what to do after the MBA and was drawn to strategy, I went to work for Arthur D. Little in Madrid and Boston, but then decided to move back to Europe to join the Automotive Practice of A.T. Kearney.

If you are at the earlier stages of your career, then it is fine to add more context about where you came from, what you studied and why you made the first initial choices in your professional life.

If the real reason you took your first job was to see the world or move out of your family's house, then that needs to be part of the story too. When saying things like this, however, the third idea is to think about how to say things such that they cast the best light possible. Instead of explaining, for example, that your family was dysfunctional in some way and you had to get out of there, you might say that you craved your own independence. It's still true but sounds better.

The fourth idea goes deeper and has to do with the reasons for changes. This is especially true for negative experiences such as getting laid off or fired. I have spoken with a number of managers who appear to have changed jobs every 12–24 months and tell the story in such a way as it is never their fault when things did not work out.

Their story is always about how each opportunity was not what it was sup-posed to be or a specific executive had a style that the person could not live with, and so on.

Often people who have lost their job tell the story with a deep sense of betrayal, hurt or anger. While these emotions may be completely justified, they will not help you get another job.

Going back to the metaphor about the race, losing a job is the equivalent of falling in the *rough* or running into a tree. When I was a headhunter, I would ask people who had a string of such experiences if they were unlucky or had bad judgment. Nothing else could explain a string of four or five different failures in a row.

The situation is completely different when the story has a different tone and you put yourself and your own mistakes at the heart of the issue. When we take responsibility for what happens around us, it opens us up to learning from our mistakes. The fifth idea that will help with telling the story is to make learning a central theme.

If you were to say that you did not properly evaluate an opportunity or failed to see the type of person your future boss was before taking a job, then I could see that you had learned something from your experience and may be ready to succeed the next time.

When I was a headhunter, I would write up my candidates' careers in terms of the steps they had made along the way. For each step I would explain why they took a specific job, what they accomplished and learned in the position and why they left. While people tend to focus on accomplishments, what really makes a story interesting is personal growth.

Sometimes I can see that someone is still emotionally tied to a position that they had lost and needs time to process what has happened before they will be able to tell the story in a more positive way.

This might involve coming to terms with their own shortcomings on how they did not pay enough attention to some political aspect of the situation or the coming market downturn. It's hard work and at times I advise people to go away to the mountains or the sea for a few days and come back when they are ready.

Where the metaphors come in is that may make it easier to articulate your own story.

If you want to make a clear break with your current line of work, for example, then the river may be helpful as it allows you to talk about past experiences in a positive way but also to work in the idea that this profession is simply taking you to the wrong place.

If on the other hand you have recently had an important setback and run into a metaphorical tree, then it might make sense to explain how you were so focused on getting results that you did not realize that there was a larger, political dimension which you failed to manage.

In the end, your personal story needs to be both true and compelling.

Typically, we can craft such a story when looking back even if the changes seemed more chaotic when we were actually making them. The reason this is so critical is that whatever happens next needs to somehow flow from what came before. This change may be gradual or abrupt but needs to be well articulated.

The sixth idea is to be culturally sensitive. Americans often speak proudly about their accomplishments, but this is much less common in many European and Asian countries where "blowing your own horn" is considered unseemly. Making an important move for family reasons may be considered as proof of integrity in one place but not in another.

My last advice is to take care how to treat the economic damage done by the virus and its role in your own story. The positive aspect is that this crisis has affected many businesses and the people who work in them so if this is your case, you are not alone. The difficult part, however, is that it is still important to take responsibility for your own situation and talk about what you learned as a result of the situation.

Even when you have been impacted by large events such as Covid-19, automoation or Russia's invasion of Ukraine, I encourage you to still find a way to take some repsonsbility for your present situation. After returning to Western Europe a Russian friend, for example, told me that he never imagined that his governement would invade Ukraine and that he ignored some of the warning signs.

Once the past is clear it is possible to begin the process of looking ahead to the next step and sometimes the story itself will indicate what should logically come next.

Imagining Your Future

In my experience, most people spend little time trying to imagine what the future will look like. When they do, they typically rely on magic, hope, faith or forecasts.

Magic is defined as the use of spells or other means to harness supernatural forces which have an effect on the physical world. In terms of looking into the future people use Tarot cards, crystal balls and the throwing of I-ching trigrams just to name a few.

While I try to keep an open mind about such things, I do not recommend that you plan your professional future based on magic although I do believe that skilled practitioners can read people well and may be able to give you insights into your deepest hopes and desires. I am also convinced that a deep study of the I-ching, Kabala or other ancient texts can also bring insight and wisdom.

Hope is defined as wanting something to happen or be true. In my view many of the books which extoll the benefits of the coming revolution in technology and the future of work fit clearly in this category.

What is clear is that advanced digital technology holds the promise to free people from drudgery and bring about a utopian world. The future may belong to those people who get with the program, move from gig to gig and maximize their perceived value through constant self-promotion on social media. The thing is that just wishing for a future does not make it so, and there are signs that things will be more complicated.

Faith is normally associated with a deep belief in god and the religious rituals that often accompany such conviction. In this context I refer to people's faith in very specific futures about which they are completely convinced. Some people are very optimistic about how all the trends discussed in Chapter 1 will play out, and others are convinced we are heading for an environmental and/ or economic disaster and that there is little humanity can do to avoid the coming apocalypse.

Forecasting uses statistical methods to estimate what things may look like at some future point in time. The basic idea is that if we know what the past was, we can extend a line to the future following the trend. Forecasting is a legitimate science and many businesses, governments and global agencies devote enormous amount of attention to it. The problem is that forecasting has important limits, and one of them is that it has a hard time dealing with multiple variables, feedback loops and discontinuities.

Forecasting, for example, missed the pandemic and other big changes to the world like the explosion of smartphones, tablets, apps, the pervasiveness of social media platforms, the rise of China, the financial crisis of 2008–2009 and, of course, COVID-19.

Scenario Planning

The starting point for scenario development is that the future will be very different and that it *cannot* be known. The purpose of using the technique is to explore what *might* happen, as opposed to trying and figuring out what *will* happen. Once possibilities are identified, it is then possible to make plans based on those different possibilities.

In business, the use of scenario planning was pioneered by Shell and in the political arena it was used to great effect in South Africa's transition from apartheid to majority rule.

Interestingly, the World Health Organization actually ran a simulation in 2018 on what they called Virus X. The idea was to think about what would happen if a previously unknown virus would sweep across the world.

In building different scenarios the idea is to use your imagination and construct futures for the world that you think make sense and then see how your professional choices will evolve in the different futures.

You may find a path which is essentially future proof as you can see it playing out positively in all the possibilities you imagine. Alternatively, you may also discover inflection points that you need to pay close attention to as the future unfolds.

Will the world be rich or poor? At peace or engulfed in war? How will different countries, regions and cities fare in the future? How will industries change and companies come and go?

While some may say the future is too uncertain, I believe that we can make some educated guesses about its direction which can help us make decisions about what to do. I strongly believe, furthermore, that not thinking ahead is fundamentally irresponsible especially if you have a family that depends on you.

Scenario planners look at medium-term trends or what they call drivers to flesh out alternative scenarios for the future. I recommend looking at the four trends discussed in Chapter 1 as well adding additional trends which are particularly relevant to you.

For someone who is looking at health care, for example, AI and robotics will certainly be important but so will the overall regulatory framework as well as progress in the life sciences and the demographic make-up of a specific location.

Another important aspect in scenario planning is to use a time frame which is far enough in the future for the trends to play out yet not so far away that the entire exercise starts to look like science fiction. Generally speaking, I do not recommend trying to construct scenarios beyond the next 15–20 years as most of us will have a hard time thinking that far ahead.

I suggest you construct two or perhaps three scenarios to show how the different trends could potentially combine to create different futures. The final step is to tie the future scenarios back to the present by developing a narrative for how each scenario will come to be during the time frame imagined.

You can then use the scenarios to extend your story into the future and see how a selection of *space*, *role* and *place* will fit into it.

Key Ideas Chapter 3

- You need to be able to clearly articulate your personal story.
- Your professional path may resemble either a trip downriver or an adventure race across different terrain over time.
- There are seven ideas for telling your story which will make it more compelling:
    1. It must be true,
    2. It should be interesting and short,
    3. How you tell it is as important as what you say,
    4. Only by taking responsibility do we learn from misfortune and mistakes,
    5. The most compelling stories focus on learning and personal growth,
    6. Stories may require some cultural adaptation,
    7. The pandemic, the invasion of Ukraine, or some other major event may be part of your story.
- Scenario planning is the best way of looking far into the future and you may want to develop two to three different scenarios.

CHAPTER 4

SHAPING THE SPACE

Although you can start in any of the three dimensions, I normally start a conversation with people by asking them about their choice of *space*. In the past, I referred to this part of the framework as industry or sector, meaning automotive, financial services, consumer goods, and so on.

The reason to start with this idea is that the professional world has always been organized in this way. In medieval times the craftsmen of Europe had guilds for the different trades and professions. Likewise, the great cities of the middle ages had specific districts for the metalworkers, carpet makers, fruit sellers, and so on, and you can still get a feel for what that was like in some places such as the old city of Marrakesh in Morocco.

Even today, people who work in a similar or related area identify with one another and often know each other in a specific geography. They congregate at the same events and often have similar problems to overcome. They may even share a worldview or way of looking at things.

Back in the 1990s, for example, as a consultant to the automotive industry, I went to the Detroit Auto Show every year. The show takes place in early January, and while the weather normally consists of snow, freezing rain or both, it is the heart of the North American automotive industry.

All the senior executives go to the press days which happen just before the show is open to the general public, and for me it was a great opportunity to meet with my clients. In Europe a similar event takes place in Geneva.

Besides the auto show itself, there were a series of parallel events, and attendance was a sure sign that you were part of the overall community. For a few years, for example, Chrysler would hold a cocktail reception at the nearby firehouse and raise money for the Detroit Firefighters.

During those years of my professional life I defined myself as being part of the automotive industry. Even though my *role* was a management consultant, my allegiance was to the community of clients and contacts that I would meet with in Detroit and Geneva. I felt at home with these people and could talk about their issues and problems.

Over the last few years, however, the idea of an industry or sector has been losing its value. Automotive, for example, is rapidly evolving as new forms of car ownership are becoming popular and as new ways from getting from place to place are emerging.

Today people in that business talk about mobility. I use the word "space" as it goes beyond industry and is broad enough to cover most fields. Using this language, the mobility *space* is broader than the automotive sector.

Blurring Lines

Beyond automotive, the lines between many traditional industry sectors are blurring and overlapping. Even the standard codes used to describe the economy such as SIC or NAICS appear to be out of step with where things are going (see Box 4).

BOX 4: SIC(K) CODES

There is an industrial coding system in the United States and many western countries called SIC codes. The codes were established in 1937 and then revised by the office of management and budget of the US Congress in 1987 to reflect the modernization that the economy had gone through over those 50 years.

As a result of the North American Free Trade Agreement in 1994 a new set of codes was established called the North American Industrial Classification System (NAICS). The NAICS was last updated in 2017.

NAICS allows you to characterize a business using a six-digit code which indicates broad industrial sectors, subsectors, industry groups, industries and a final level which makes distinctions between parts of an industry such as between dog and cat food manufacturing (code 311111) and other animal food manufacturing (311119).

All together the NAICS codes cover 20 industrial sectors which can then be divided into 1057 different business areas at the final level.

One of the values of such coding system is that it makes possible to calculate statistics on the changes happening to the economy as a whole. Using data from the US Bureau of Economic Analsysis,[1] for example, it is possible to compare the make-up of the economy in 2017 with that of 1997.

---

1   BEA.Gov, accessed October 20, 2019.

Over those 20 years, manufacturing decreased from accounting for 25.3 percent of gross domestic output to 17.1 percent. Over the same time period finance and insurance rose from 5.7 percent to 7.3 percent and health care services from 5.6 to 6.9 percent.

One problem with the codes, however, is that many businesses and marketing companies continue to use the SIC codes while others and the governments of the U.S., Canada, and Mexico have switched to NAICS.

Another problem is that due to the blurring of lines between sectors and the evolution of technology and business models, the codes are increasingly becoming difficult to use or perhaps even getting in the way of having meaningful discussions.

While it is necessary to continue to use the codes for reporting to the government, in thinking about what to do with your professional life, I suggest using the idea of *space*, and urge you to make up your own classification of the global economy which makes sense to you.

NAICS 2017 Structure

Sector	Name	Subsectors (3-digit)	Industry Groups (4-digit)	NAICS Industries (5-digit)	Final Level (6-digit)
11	Agriculture, Forestry, Fishing and Hunting	5	19	42	64
21	Mining, Quarrying, and Oil and Gas Extraction	3	5	11	28
22	Utilities	1	3	6	14
23	Construction	3	10	28	31
31-33	Manufacturing	21	86	180	360
42	Wholesale Trade	3	19	71	71
44-45	Retail Trade	12	27	57	66
48-49	Transportation and Warehousing	11	29	42	57
51	Information	6	11	25	31
52	Finance and Insurance	5	11	31	41
53	Real Estate and Rental and Leasing	3	8	17	24
54	Professional, Scientific, and Technical Services	1	9	35	49
55	Management of Companies and Enterprises	1	1	1	3
56	Administrative and Support and Waste Management and Remediation Services	2	11	29	44

Sector	Name	Subsectors (3-digit)	Industry Groups (4-digit)	NAICS Industries (5-digit)	Final Level (6-digit)
61	Educational Services	1	7	12	17
62	Health Care and Social Assistance	4	18	30	39
71	Arts, Entertainment, and Recreation	3	9	23	25
72	Accomodation and Food Services	2	6	10	15
81	Other Services [except Public Administration)	4	14	30	49
92	Public Administration	8	8	29	29
	Total	**99**	**311**	**709**	**1057**

When I speak about blurring lines, I also mean that it is increasingly difficult to tell one business from another. One of the main reasons for this is how different technologies are beginning to overlap with each other. This trend is normally called technological convergence and is particularly evident in the impact of computers and digitalization in many sectors of the economy.

Media, for example, used to consist of a number of sectors such as magazines, newspapers, television, film, and so on. I saw this firsthand when I was the academic director of a program for media executives that IESE Business School offered in New York and Los Angeles.

At the beginning of the program each participant felt that they faced unique challenges in their segment of the business. We typically had people from television, radio, newspapers and the movie business. After spending time together, however, each of the participants realized that they were facing many of the same challenges brought about by the digitalization and globalization of the larger media *space*.

Digital technology has had a tremendous impact on all types of media businesses. These changes are due to reducing production costs, while at the same time, increasing competition and disrupting distribution channels and allowing for the emergence of a number of new business models. All of this has served to blur the lines between these businesses which had, once upon a time, very distinct characteristics.

Another example of a *space* in the lines are blurring the lines in mobile communications. Over the last few years the most important trade fair for that *space* has become the one in Barcelona held every March called the World Mobile

Congress. Although it was canceled in 2020 and hybrid in 2021, the MWC normally attracts more than 100,000 people and goes well beyond the cell phone industry as such. The event brings in companies making cell phones and equipment but also content providers, app developers and virtually the entire set of businesses that uses or depends on the technology.

Besides innovation in digital technology, other technologies are converging. Food producers are striving to make their products more nutritious and connected to physical well-being. This is leading to the emergence of a category called foodceuticals or food products which contain vitamins and other ingredients blurring the lines been the food business and the pharmaceutical industry.

A former student in the dairy business in Ireland, for example, considers milk to be a delivery mechanism for supplements and offers different milk products that are enriched with protein, iron and natural additives that reduce cholesterol to name a few.

In addition to technological convergence, the lines between industries are also blurring as consumers become accustomed to features they experience in one business that they then demand from others. Amazon and Amazon Prime, for example, have taught us that we can get basically anything delivered to our homes in a short time so now more and more products and services are being delivered to us at the touch of an app.

Companies such as Good Eats in the United States and Rappi in Latin America have cut across traditional lines of business and have created a new *space* which combines aspects of package delivery and goes beyond the traditional food delivery model that was connected to pizza or Chinese restaurants. This trend to home delivery and consumption has also leapt ahead of its forecasts as a result of the pandemic.

In another example, before the pandemic hit, movie theaters were increasingly behaving like bars and restaurants even delivering drinks and snacks to your seat while the show is playing. The pandemic has, of course, hit the theater industry extremely hard and put into question its very survival.

Part of this general blurring of industries is a result of companies looking to continue to grow despite having already high market shares and relatively low growth in their core business.

This has led to companies going well beyond the traditional idea of line extensions into businesses that you would really not have thought possible. I recently bought, for example, a charging cable for a phone made by a leading battery manufacturer. This is an example of a battery company redefining their industry as the charging *space* and using their brand equity in a way that was surprising to me.

Blurring is also happening because traditional industries are being attacked by start-ups and other firms who are playing by different rules. The common language talks about industry disruption in which new business models upset the old order of things making it difficult for companies which have been in business for years to react in time.

Often such disruption comes from changing distribution networks or cutting out distributors, wholesalers or even retailers and going directly to consumers. You see such disruption going on in the fintech *space* with literally thousands of new companies trying to figure out how to take business away from traditional banks and insurance companies.

In many ways 2020 has accelerated the rate of change on many of these trends further blurring the lines between different industries.

Defining the *Space*

While the lines between businesses are blurring, what is also important, however, is to bear in mind that older people came of age at another time and place and may still have mental models defined when each sector and subsector had its own rules and a relatively stable structure.

Many of these people still play leading roles in a number of companies and may be uncomfortable with or even actively resist the changes around them. They may simply not get it if you talk to them about some emerging *space*, while their view of the world is still locked in by their training and experience.

It is important, therefore, to strike a balance between using the concept of *space* to open up new possibilities while keeping enough focus so that you can connect with specific people who see themselves as working in the same parts of the economy, go to the same trade shows and other types of events, use the same language and jargon or even wear the same types of clothes. While this might be a bit confusing, I suggest you use the idea of *space* to figure out what you want to do but be ready to talk about the sector or industry.

Some people use the term "ecosystem," which has its roots in biology, to get at the idea of the larger *space*. All the plants, fish and creatures in a tide pool, for example, belong to the same ecosystem. The term is often applied to the digital world as it can include all kinds of actual and potential players.

Organizations which are suppliers, customers or competitors of each other could be said to occupy the same ecosystem. While I use this idea for developing business strategy, I find it potentially too broad for choosing what to do. The digital economy, for example, is much too broad a definition, and while you may want to be part of that overall ecosystem, I think a more concrete definition of *space* is needed.

An example of this process of subdivision can be seen at Web Summit which attracts about 70,000 people from all over the world to Lisbon in a normal year. While Web Summit does have keynote speeches in the 15,000-seat Altice Arena, most of the action happens in smaller subsections which are focused on things like financial services (Fintech), environmental sustainability (Planet Tech) and about a dozen other topics within the overall digital ecosystem.

The idea is therefore to define the *space* you want to be a part of taking into account change and the blurring lines between different sectors while still having enough focus to reach the right people.

Drawing on the section devoted to passion in Chapter 2, what products or services are you really interested in? What service, product or technology can keep you motivated day after day and month after month?

Another way to tackle the question is to focus on customers. If you think about one specific set of business customers or consumers, you could drill down into a specific set of needs they have as a way of defining a *space*. Harvard's Clay Christensen defined this approach as focusing on the job to be done. His famous example is that we really do not need to own an electric drill but do need to make a hole in the wall from time to time.

A good definition of *space* will lend itself naturally to being part of a compelling story. If, in other words, it is not possible to explain the *space* you are interested in a simple and straightforward way, then you should probably redefine it and try again. You will have to explain it to people who "get it" as well as others who may need such an explanation to really understand what you are looking for and how they can help you.

A Problem to Solve

Robert "Hutch" Hutchinson is an entrepreneur and Sr. Fellow at the Rocky Mountain Institute who focusses on the environmental sustainability of buildings. Hutch had actually spent the first 20 years of his career opening offices all over the world for the Boston Consulting Group and then decided to move his family to Boulder and joined the institute to make a positive contribution and restore some sense of balance to his life.

The way Hutch formulated the choice of *space* was by asking my students which problem did they want to help solve? By problem he did not refer to the job to be done by some segment of consumers or business customers but larger more complex issues which affects millions of people or the planet itself. Working on such issues could potentially absorb any number of years of your career or even be the focus of your life's work.

For Hutch, large, complex issues such as reducing the cost of solar power or developing sustainable transportation can give clarity of purpose regardless of the changing times and blurring lines between sectors. Hutch's view is that each one of us has the opportunity to focus on two or three different problems in the course of our lives.

Focusing on the problem gives a different perspective as to which companies or subsectors belong to the same *space*.

The transition to a low carbon economy touches directly, for example, on a number of different parts of the energy business but also has to do with energy efficiency and the decarbonization of a number of materials and industrial processes.

One could, for example, say I am looking at the energy efficiency *space* in order to help with the decarbonization of the energy mix, since buildings currently consume 40 percent of all energy and improvement of 50 percent would reduce the primary demand for energy by 20 percent. This can be achieved through better electrical systems in people's homes as well as improved insulation and windows, more use of heat pumps, and so on.

You can take this approach on any large problem that you might be passionate about including health care access, economic inequality, nutrition, wellness or any other issue.

The idea is to think about all of the different companies, government agencies and organizations in civil society which are involved or may be involved in making progress on such an issue and developing your own definition of *space* around that idea.

Many such big problems are also connected to a specific region, country or part of the world. Someone might work to eliminate illiteracy in a specific country or work on helping people gain access to clean water or energy. The reality is that the world has plenty of big problems to fix and the United Nations has identified 17 Sustainable Development Goals which could be a source of inspiration (see Box 11).

This approach can be effective since that many of the people involved in such an effort actually do know one another, go to the same conferences and read the same specialized publications and therefore can be approached using the networking techniques that are discussed in Chapter 9.

Another point is that addressing important problems does not necessarily mean giving up a relatively high salary or joining a nonprofit organization. In the first place there are many people in the public and nonprofit sector who do actually make reasonable money. United Nations employees, for example, not only make reasonable salaries but also are exempted from income tax.

Second, there are many ways to get involved in big problems including fundraising, social entrepreneurship and for-profit business. Social entrepreneurship is normally defined as building a business which has a social objective as its primary purpose. Such companies normally do strive to make a profit but do not place financial objectives first.

Focusing on a big problem is also very useful in making your own story more powerful and compelling due to your knowledge about the topic and passion for it.

Tomorrow's Spaces

The last piece of the puzzle is to think about how the *space* you are interested in will evolve over time ideally developing scenarios as discussed in Chapter 3.

Back in 1985, I was a young MBA student and had the good fortune to study strategy with Professor Harry Hansen, who had taught at the Harvard Business School through most of the 1960s and 1970s.

One afternoon, a group of us followed Professor Hansen up to his office, and one of my colleagues asked him if there was any way to tell beforehand which of his students would go on to do great things in their careers.

According to Hansen, the MBA students who went farthest were neither the brightest nor the hardest working. They were not the ones who talked the most in class or kept quiet and listened. They were not even the organizers of clubs and social activities. None of these categories had any correlation in his view with long-term business success and neither did any combination of looks, gender, race or religion. The only thing that had a clear correlation over the long term was the industry or sector that people chose to go into after school or at some later point in their career.

Hansen's message was essentially that the *space* one chooses determines, to a large degree, the amount of opportunity you will have. I have seen the same happen with my own students and friends over the years.

To go back to the metaphor of the river, some rivers move faster than others. The flow of water might increase as a result of the changing climate or run dry. The thing is that whether you paddle hard or just float along, much of your speed will be determined by the environment you are in.

So, what are some of the *spaces* that might be relevant over the next 10–20 years, and how might they be defined? I will discuss 10 spaces that I personally think are interesting as examples of how this idea can be brought to life. They are based on a combination of my own reading of the tea leaves and the things which strike my attention.

Please do not be concerned if the *space* you are interested does not appear in my list. The point of sharing some thought on these is to stimulate your own ideas about how to define a space that appeals to you and how it may evolve in the future. These *spaces* also overlap in some ways which goes back to the point that a *space* is what you define it to be, and the test is whether you can explain it to other people.

1) Clean energy

The first *space* that I think will be of interest has to do with the transition to a low carbon economy which I believe will happen over the next 10 to 20 years. While politicians in different countries might slow things down or speed things up, in the medium term, the world has no choice but to solve this problem.

In this *space* I would include companies which finance, manufacture and manage the renewable and distributed energy infrastructure that the world will need to deal with the threat of climate change.

This includes manufacturers of solar panels and wind turbines and the companies building the electrical infrastructure needed to rebuild power grids and manage distributed energy networks. It also includes a large number of HVAC technicians, plumbers and electricians who will be involved in making our buildings and homes more energy efficient.

There is enormous amount of software and AI needed in this field, and I would also include specialized engineering outfits and start-ups into the overall *space*.

The advantage of the *space* is that in the long term I think it is a sure bet. The disadvantage is the timing of particular aspects of the *space*, such as the rate of deployment of offshore wind, in specific places or geographies can be uncertain depending on the politics of a given country or territory.

2) Health care

According to the Bureau of Labor Statistics, 14 percent of the American work-force is involved in health care not including people who work in government-owned hospitals and clinics. The cost of health care has skyrocketed over the last 20 years, and the industry is in dire need of radical change. The experience of 2020 has only made it more apparent that the overall system is in need of a drastic overhaul.

Advanced medical devices, computer-facilitated breakthroughs in new drugs and other advanced technologies also offer tremendous promise in the years to come.

Digital technology is also finding its way into the sector, and AI offers enormous possibilities across the value chain of the *space* running from drug development to diagnosis and dosage control.

I recently had a conversation with a young man who was trying to get into medical school, and I asked him if perhaps studying computer science would be a better way to prepare for the future of health care.

The advantage of this *space* is that it is critically important for the humanity and the world. The challenge is that things are changing quickly, and it may be difficult to know which aspect of the *space* to get involved with.

3) Clean mobility

Although gas-guzzling and polluting cars may become a thing of the past, people will still need to get from place to place. Electric and hybrid cars, vehicles powered by hydrogen fuel cells and hyperefficient internal combustion engines will most likely coexist in the future with clean mass transit options. Add the ride-sharing/taxi business, as well as other forms of personal transportation such as the now-ubiquitous electric scooters, and you begin to define the emerging *space* of clean mobility.

One thing that is driving this shift is the improved performance and lower cost of batteries which power all kinds of electric vehicles. Another is increasing concern about air pollution in cities which has resulted in a ban on diesel engines which is scheduled to take effect in many cities in the world including London and Paris in 2025. Concern about climate change is also driving this trend, although electric power does need to be generated in one way or another.

4) Manufacturing 4.0

Manufacturing industries are also going through a technological revolution which includes increased and new forms of automation, digitally connecting all aspects of factories and 3D printing. The new capabilities allow for smaller lot sizes, increased traceability and potentially a lower environmental footprint.

Like in many other parts of the economy, the manufacturing *space* is opening up new career paths and specialization opportunities, while, at the same time, cutting down on the need for repetitive labor. Another driver of the trend to move toward even more industrial automation is the fact that robots do not get sick.

As these technologies make their way into the world there will be enormous opportunities to speed up their dissemination as those firms which do not manage the transition may find themselves out of the competitive race.

5) Sustainable consumption

Another very exciting *space* will be bioplastics and other elements of a circular economy. If you think this is crazy talk, The Coca-Cola Company has already made itself neutral in terms of water usage in 2015 and has made a public commitment to achieving zero waste by 2030!

One scenario that I think is very possible is for concern about the environmental impact of all goods and services to increase over time touching on supply chain management as well as marketing and distribution.

In the 1950s and 1960s, for example, the world largely phased out returnable bottles for disposable cans and plastic containers. My guess is that plastic will be phased out over time and returnable containers will make a comeback as will other aspects of the circular economy.

6) Digital commerce, fulfillment and the future of retail

Digital technology has had an enormous impact on retail. In the first 20 years of bar code technology, for example, retailers became more powerful than the brands as they were able to harness the data available to them and have better control of their own inventories.

That benefit, however, is now moving to platforms such as Amazon, Alibaba and others as the transformation of the retail business has also been accelerated by the pandemic. Physical retailing is also in the process of transformation due to technological change allowing for increased automation in stores.

I would add order fulfillment to a definition of this *space* as e-commerce does not work without delivery services of the kind offered by UPS, Amazon and the Post Office. While normally such services would be part of the transportation and logistics industry, including them here is a good example of thinking in terms of *space* as it is all interdependent.

UPS itself was actually started back in Seattle in 1907, and its legendary founder, Jim Casey, built the business by delivering packages for retail stores. Today Amazon is both a serious competitor to UPS and its largest customer.

7) Gaming and entertainment

One of the clear trends over the last few years has been the explosion of all types of entertainment from gaming to music to television and film. In an increasingly automated world, it makes sense that people will have more time to play, watch and listen. In the postvirus world, people will also value the ability to pursue their hobbies and passions without leaving their house or apartment.

Clearly, the distribution of content has been changing and will continue to evolve over the next 10–20 years, but regardless of whether it is boxed, broadcast or streamed, more people will likely spend more time on developed content in the future.

This opens up opportunities for artists of all kinds, including directors, actors set designers, and so on, all types of technical people and the businesspeople who can finance the production and distribution of that content.

8) Cybersecurity

With the digitalization of much of the industrial and social fabric of society comes enormous vulnerabilities at different levels. This has already sparked the growth of the *space* to over $180 billion in 2021 with double-digit growth.[2]

The challenge in defining this *space* has to do with how much it intersects with all other aspects of the digital environment. There are, however, a clear set of players focused on different aspects of the problem including financial institutions, critical infrastructure, business in general, consumers, government and the military.

9) Space, aerospace and defence

If you have ever read any science fiction, you may be attracted by the explosion of activity connected with the commercialization of space which is

---

2 Grand View Research, August 2021.

undergoing a revolution. Led by well-financed companies such as SpaceX and Virgin Galactic, there are thousands of start-ups doing different things. This space also includes the traditional aerospace companies such as Boeing, Airbus, Lockheed Martin, and so on, as well as the government agencies such as NASA, the European Space Agency and the China National Space Administration just to name a few.

In addition to aerospace, the Stockholm International Peace Research Institute, world defence spending has increased by over 2 percent for the last two years, and this covers everything from traditional weaponry to new, advanced robotics and exotic weapons. In a world beset by an increasingly complex and multipolar geopolitical situation and war, it is clear that this trend will continue.

10) Smart cities and resilience

One of the biggest trends on a global basis is the increasing number of people living in the world's cities. Digitalization and the need to make these cities more sustainable are driving a number of improvements in the way cities are organized, managed and maintained.

The idea of smart cities includes technologies such as mass transit, increased electrification and the deployment of sensors as well as the deployment of 5G telecommunications. The idea also includes concepts of urban governance, social innovation and city planning.

Cities will also suffer the negative impacts of climate change leading to increased demand for coastal defences, air and water purification, and vertical farming.

Key Ideas Chapter 4

- Although the lines between industries are blurring, the world's economy is still largely divided between different areas of human activity which eventually boils down to products and services.
- One way of thinking about these areas is as *spaces* of human endeavor. The idea of *space* takes into account technological and business model innovation but does require some imagination and conceptual clarity.
- Another way of arriving at a specific *space* is to think about those organizations involved in solving some of the world's most pressing problems.

- Ten spaces that will, most likely, be areas of opportunity in the future include
  1. Clean energy,
  2. Health care,
  3. Clean mobility,
  4. Manufacturing 4.0,
  5. Sustainable consumption,
  6. Digital commerce, fulfillment and the future of retail,
  7. Gaming and entertainment,
  8. Cybersecurity,
  9. Space, aerospace and defense,
  10. Smart cities and resilience.

CHAPTER 5

CHOOSING A ROLE

Like industries, job titles are also changing due to a number of factors including new business models, forms of organization and automation. I prefer to use the term "role" instead of job or position as it gets at the heart of what it is that you do to add value in an organization.

This idea is particularly important in the postvirus world as many assumptions about the way people work have been changed by our collective experience during the pandemic. We have found, for example, that much more can be achieved working remotely than most of us ever thought was possible. While it is unclear where all of this is going, what we already know is that we cannot take for granted the structure of the organizations we have up until now.

Some *roles* will fade away, and others emerge in the new normal. To be sure that your *role* will be part of the future, you must focus on the ways you create value. Another way to say this is that each one of us has to bring something to the party if we want to get invited back.

You might find that my focus on value as opposed to meaning or passion is too cold or heartless, but these ideas are discussed in other parts of the book. When thinking about different *roles*, it is critical that you honestly and objectively identify what the value of that *role* might be in a particular *space* and at a particular *place* and time.

I do not, by the way, limit value to money. The music and film teacher at our local high school, for example, had an enormous impact on both my daughters when they were his students. His value in the community is, in my view, enormous, and in general I feel we do not pay teachers enough.

A *role* might be about teaching, developing new science, applying existing technology or have to do with connecting ideas and people. It could also be about working in sales or doing something else to help a business function such as managing its financial position, finding and retaining people or providing some of the other services needed in today's complex society.

You may be satisfied by the *role* that you have been doing or what you have been trained to do. On the other hand, you may feel that you are in a specific *role* as if by accident and have a strong desire to make a change.

I started my own career as an engineer and thought that by going to business school I could change my *role* and go into business development or sales. After school, I became a management consultant which was a *role* that I did not even know existed when I was an engineer.

Today there is a demand for *roles* that did not exist just a few years ago such as community manager, and more change is likely to occur over the next 5, 10 and 20 years.

Changing Structures

Once upon a time, jobs could be interchangeable with *roles*. The industrial fabric of society was evolving slowly, if at all. Job titles, and what those titles meant, were very stable.

Companies were typically organized along functional or geographic lines with senior managers being responsible for large areas of the business or specific states, countries or regions. In these structures, you typically worked in sales, marketing, production management, engineering, financial control or whatever other function you had begun working in at the start of your career.

In large, international companies, there would be a country manager at the top who would, in turn, have a functional organization reporting to them. In either case, *roles* were fairly straightforward and obeyed a progression over time.

In large consumer marketing firms, such as Procter & Gamble, a young executive would start out as an assistant brand manager and work their way up to becoming brand manager and then group brand manager receiving promotions every few years. They might be the brand manager for a relatively small product and then be promoted to a larger, more critical product or category with the same title but a larger advertising budget and more responsibility. In any case the *role* of a marketing manager was similar and fairly well-defined across most of the large, consumer product companies.

What I have seen in the last few years, however, is massive change across all aspects of society and particularly in the business world. As companies evolve and adapt to changing circumstance and technology, they are also adopting new organizational models which have very different roles.

The country manager role has, for example, disappeared in many companies and been replaced by a matrix organization with heads of global business units, central functions and large regional territories such as Asia Pacific, EMEA or the Americas.

Many companies have also implemented shared service centers which do much of the back-office work in central locations. In many cases, these are managed by other companies all together.

An even newer organizational model has emerged in software and internet companies and is normally referred to as the agile organization.

Recognizing how slow functional and matrix structures can become, agile organizations are based around units of people who collectively have the expertise needed to accomplish specific tasks and are left to do it.

To get at the very different *roles* that people play, agile structures come with a new vocabulary. Departments and department heads are done away with and replaced with tribes, and project teams adopt scrum methods (see Box 5).

BOX 5: TRIBES AND SCRUMS

In 2004, Tom Malone, a professor at the Sloan School at MIT published a book titled *The Future of Work*. His insight, which predated much of the work in this area is that as the cost of telecommunications goes down and access to information goes up, a new form of organization will develop.

Agile began as a way of organizing software projects to get to market faster. The basic idea was to co-locate all of the people necessary to come up with a new idea, develop its requirements, write and test the code and get it into the market.

The idea of Agile has now moved beyond programming and is rapidly becoming a way of organizing companies and even a philosophy of management. At its heart is the idea that semi-autonomous teams can get on with their work as long as they have all of the relevant functions in the team.

To highlight its differences with other ways of organizing companies and teams, new language is used. *Scrum*, for example, is a word taken from rugby and is defined as a process framework used to management product development and other knowledge work.[1] The values of a team using

---

1 agilealliance.org, accessed February 18, 2020.

scrum would include commitment, courage, focus, opens, and respect. Typically scrum is used when developing successive versions of a product in rapid succession.

Tribes are typically groups of people with a particular business knowledge. In a traditional organization they may have been grouped into a department with a department head but in an agile section they will be dispersed in a number of teams and would only come together for sharing knowledge and celebrating successes.

There are many organizations which are currently trying to take the lessons learned in the agile programming movement and then to apply them across a wide variety of organizations and settings.

In developing new digital products and software, a number of companies such as Spotify, Google and a host of smaller start-ups have implemented Agile in their programming teams. A large European bank that we train, for example, has implemented agile in order to align the entire company around customer-facing activities in an effort to become faster and more innovative.

With the new technologies and the experience of 2020, physical proximity becomes less important. These evolving structures were actually predicted by Tom Malone in 2004. For Malone, management exists because there is friction in communications. As that friction goes away, organizations can become much flatter and new *roles* can emerge while others go away.

Roles Not Jobs

Regardless of whether you find yourself in a functional organization, a matrix structure or an agile unit or company, the key is to be clear about what *role* you are playing, the value it adds and why you want to play that *role* in that particular *space*.

I once had a student who was deeply concerned about climate change and asked that I introduce him to a friend of mine who was the CEO of a company involved in developing and trading carbon credits in the early 2000s. The company was growing, and the CEO needed as many good people as he could find.

The business was about developing alternative energy projects in developing countries, certifying them and then trading the carbon credits that were created.

At my request the CEO met with my student but couldn't find a *role* for him to play. Although the student was passionate about carbon trading, he did not want to work at the trading desk. He also was not ready to go off to developing countries to develop the projects or do the administrative and legal work needed to get the credits approved.

The lesson from the story is that identifying the *space* that you want to be a part of is not enough. It is also necessary to drill down and figure out what you are actually going to do once you get there!

Within a given *space* there are a number of different subjects or topics. Which ones do you want to deal with? In the example above my student had not thought through if he would rather be on the development side, the legal aspects or the trading desk? You can also look at the more classic functional areas in a business such as finance, marketing, sales or HR to get a sense of the different subjects which lead to *roles*.

Another former student has been the HR person for several start-ups in Silicon Valley. Her particular *role* has been to recruit the first 100–200 people in the company. After doing this a couple of times she has established a reputation in the Valley and made a small fortune in the process.

Perhaps even before discussing what *role* to play, a deeper question is why to do it in the first place? What is the deeper purpose behind the *role*? The student mentioned in the example above gets a deep satisfaction from the process of helping entrepreneurs make their ideas real.

One aspect of a *role* is to look at the connections that are required to perform it. Who will you need to communicate with and with what frequency? The finance director of a growing company, for example, spends much of their time talking to the firm's bankers and backers.

Another is understanding what type of data you will be looking at. Sticking with the finance director, that job is all about keeping track of the numbers and avoiding surprises. Understanding all of the costs, payment terms, profit margins, and so on, is not everyone's idea of fun, but it is the lifeblood of business and someone needs to be on top of it.

A related question is how unique and uniquely human is your relationship to the data. Many *roles*, for example, consist essentially of speaking with people and then entering the information they acquire into a computer system and acting as a bridge between the people and the system. As systems get better at understanding natural language and as people get better at using screens and apps, many of those *roles* will disappear.

Bank tellers, gate agents, supermarket checkout people and many similar occupations are destined to either vanish or be transformed as the routine data processing aspects of these *roles* are replaced by robots, such as ATMs, mobile phones, bar code scanners and algorithms.

One of the most important questions is to determine the value of a specific *role* in a particular company or organization operating in a specific *space*. In consumer products companies, marketing people are very important. In many ways, those companies live and die by the power of their brands, and the marketing people have a very high value. In other *spaces* it might be the engineers or perhaps the finance team.

Value can also be highly dependent on the company you are involved with or even the unit in that company. As a headhunter, I became involved with Audi in Spain which sold around 20,000 cars per year in the country but was also the leading producer of advertising for Audi Europe as a whole. In the Spanish unit of Audi the advertising manager had a critical *role*.

Typically a *role* can be defined by what the essence of your work is, why you find it interesting, who you communicate with, what types of data you deal with and, finally, how you add value.

Finding Fit

What has struck me over the years is how some people seem to fit very well with their profession and others seem to struggle against what they do every day. Finding the right *role* also requires you to have a realistic and honest assessment of your skills and aptitudes as well as the life you want to live and the challenges you are willing to endure in order to get where you want to go.

Skills and aptitudes

A classmate of mine has found over the years that his own unique skill lies in developing business models around new digital ideas. He has now worked in more than a half a dozen start-ups over the years and acts as the bridge between the technologists and the marketing and sales teams.

He knows he is good at making those connections but also admits that he gets bored too easily to be the lead technical person or even last beyond 18–24 months in any given company. The key is for each of us to find something that we will be good at, enjoy, and that also fits with the life we want to lead.

In terms of physical limitations, another friend had trained to be a dentist in Europe but had not realized that he simply did not have the physical dexterity needed to manipulate the instruments until his fifth year of dentistry school, when he began to do clinical work.

At the business school, we typically encourage aspiring professors to teach a few classes before they go on to do their PhD as some people have a natural ability to stand up in front of a classroom and others will never be very good at it.

Lifestyle

Another aspect in terms of what suits us best is the lifestyle associated with different professions. Doctors and nurses, for example, work long hours and are often called upon to work nights and weekends. They have collectively lived 2020 in very difficult and dangerous conditions.

People involved with professional sports such as Major League Baseball and Formula 1 spend many weeks on the road. University professors typically enjoy more holidays than many other professionals, although we do spend some of that time grading and writing.

The point is that different *roles* normally fit better with certain lifestyles than others, and I urge you to think through how you want to live before deciding on a specific *role*. How much do you want to travel? How many hours can you/will you be happy working?

If you speak to a number of people doing a specific *role*, you will get a sense of what kind of life they live, and probably there will be some common attributes to the most successful people. Your own lifestyle will, most likely, resemble theirs assuming you are also successful.

The link between a specific *role* and the lifestyles that are compatible with it can have a huge impact on family life. Working through the trade-offs involved are absolutely essential for having a positive balance between family and work.

Realistic expectations

In the United States and most countries it is against the law to discriminate against anyone based on sex, race, religion, sexual orientation or age. The real world, however, is far from perfect, and there is evidence of certain types of people making progress to the top of specific organizations and broader *spaces*.

While this section may be considered politically incorrect, my intention is not to offend but to point out how important it is to recognize reality and deal with it in a constructive way since ethnic, racial and gender bias still exists.

In some cases, apparent discrimination is the result of a cold business logic. Consulting companies, for example, sell very expensive services to the corporate elite in a given industry or country. In many parts of the world the customers for such services come from certain regions, attend certain schools or are even members of certain families. In this case, who would you expect to get hired? A local who has all the right connections or a bright guy from some other part of the world who barely speaks the language?

At the company level there are also firms which have truly multinational and diverse management teams and others which simply do not. I often encourage people to look at the names and profiles of a company's senior executives on their website as part of their research. Do these people look like you? Do you speak the language that is spoken in the executive committee?

The idea is not to accept such practices but to acknowledge them and therefore work harder or smarter to overcome the biases that many people have.

Just do it

The point of the preceding section is not to encourage you to accept or tolerate any kind of discrimination but to urge you to take countermeasures against it assuming you have the commitment and energy to fight against such things.

Sure German is a hard language, so what? Chinese and Japanese are even harder. In some cases just the willingness to begin learning a language might produce enough of an impression to help make the difference in a specific hiring or promotion decision.

In my own career, I was lucky to be hired into a prestigious consulting firm in Madrid despite my terrible American accent and total lack of any kind of connections in the local market. The reason was that I hit it off very well with one of the senior partners who shared my love for boats. What I did for the first six months on the job was to take two hours of Spanish class each day in the early morning.

As Barcelona is a beautiful place to live, many people come there to do the MBA and then decide they want to stay. The ones that make it all manage to figure out some unique contribution they can make to the local economy, although sometimes they have to accept a somewhat reduced salary compared to what they might have made in London or New York.

What is right for you?

In my view you need to have a special mindset to be one of the few women, people of color, muslims, jews, and so on, at a certain level in an organization and either you have thick enough skin or you don't. If you do then by all means go for it as there is a special sense of triumph or value added by bringing diverse views into the decision making process of an organization and loosening it up to outside influences.

If you do not have the drive, patience and flexibility required, then perhaps look for those companies or cultures where you will be valued in part for who you are.

Sometimes people simply choose a path of lower resistance. I know many people from Europe and Asia who live and work in the United States as they are attracted to the egalitarian principals found in American businesses, research labs and academic institutions.

While prejudice still exists, American society is relatively more egalitarian and accepting than many countries of people who are different. The unlikely rise of Barack Hussein Obama is a case in point.

Are you special?

In summary, each *role* requires a different combination of skills, aptitudes and lifestyle.

In some cases, this combination is fairly common, and many people could potentially be successful in the *role*. Others, on the other hand, require very specific skills, rare aptitudes and a willingness to live life in a very specific way.

Professional athletes are an extreme case of this idea, that I call *specialness*. The concept can also be applied to surgeons, certain types of finance people and other professions.

Many years ago my immediate supervisor explained to me that if I wanted to make significant amounts of money, then I needed to focus on things that most people can't do or won't do or a combination of both. His view was that, in general, the world pays more money for professions which only a few people are able or willing to do.

There are, for example, many aspiring actors and musicians and typically such people supplement their income by waiting tables, driving for Uber or doing something else to pay the rent, while they wait for their big break. The truth is that not everyone has the combination of ability, luck and willingness to go all in to make it as a professional athlete, musician, movie star or hedge fund manager.

Does the *role* you want to play naturally fit with your skills, aptitudes and lifestyle or is it going to be a constant struggle?

This is not to say that you can never overcome your natural tendencies as there are thousands of stories of people who have overcome enormous challenges and handicaps in order to pursue their dreams. I applaud such people and find their stories truly inspiring.

What is clear, on the other hand, is that such a life is not for everyone.

My advise is to think through what you want to do, how well suited you are to it and how special you are. Only an honest assessment of such things can help you choose what to do.

You might, for example, choose to do something well within your skill set which will match your lifestyle. On the other hand, you might instead choose to reach for the stars even though you know that not everyone will get there.

Future-proof Roles

In thinking about a specific *role* I urge you to look at the value the *role* adds today and also what it is likely to be at some point in the future.

One idea is to not worry too much about what happens next and focus instead on developing the skills needed to adapt and change with whatever does come along. My guess is that not everyone will be comfortable with this approach and you might feel better in a *role* that is essentially future proof such that you will still be able to add value and therefore make a living for the foreseeable future.

Many people are concerned about how digitalization and automation are changing the nature of work. In *The Future of Success*, Robert Reich made the point in 2002 that the best jobs would go to the people who will build the digital future and the marketing types who will figure out business models to make the new ideas economically viable. He also correctly foresaw that at the high-end people will pay for human interaction and care. In this category he would place personal trainers, stylists, therapists and a whole range of concierge-level services for the wealthy.

Automation has the potential to eliminate some *roles* completely. In 2018, for example, there were 4.1 million drivers of trucks, busses and taxis, and so on, in the United States.[2] If and when autonomous vehicles are widely adopted, many if not all of the people in this *role* will need to find something else to do.

---

2 National Bureau of Labor Statistics.

Another way that digitalization and automation affects roles is by permitting machines and algorithms to take on some tasks currently done by humans changing the nature of many professions. These changes will also cut both ways as digital tools will enhance some *roles* but will also simplify others.

As was discussed in Chapter 1, the most probable scenarios involve sharp improvements in the ability of automated systems to perceive and manipulate their environment placing more and more emphasis on unique human capabilities involving creative and social intelligence.

The following are the 10 *roles* that I see as being somewhat future proof, although they will certainly evolve over time. I list them here to illustrate what I mean by the concept so you can figure out the *role* or *roles* you want to play.

1) Health care and wellness practitioner

If there is one thing that 2020 has showed us is that the health care sector is critically important. Most experts agree, however, that health care is undergoing a massive digital transformation and that many of the traditional *roles* in the industry will change as a result.

There will, however, always be *roles* to play in the health care system as patients and their families need the touch and confidence they get from other humans. One scenario has massive databases such as IBM's Watson connected to health care practitioners such that they will direct treatment based on the statistical probabilities when given patient data.

Perhaps that patient data will be recorded by increasingly sophisticated devices, but in the end humans will most likely be in the loop to interpret findings, talk to patients and administer therapies.

Interestingly enough, there are new *roles* opening up in the health care field such as an audio visual technician I met when invited to observe endoscopic (keyhole) surgery being carried out using 3D imagery. The technician was wearing a sterile surgical gown, mask and gloves and was essentially running the camera equipment and computers so that the surgeon could see what they were doing

2) Educator

Even after all of the advancements in online learning that we have seen over the last 20 years, the role of the educator is still at the heart of most educational systems and experiences. Most of us can still remember a handful of teachers who had an important impact on our lives.

Teachers form the backbone of primary and secondary education around the world and will continue to do so for many years. They do, however, need to be fully up to date in using digital technology in and outside of the classroom since many educational experiences are increasingly combining face-to-face and online elements.

As technology improves, it is likely that parts of the current educational offering will probably migrate online. The role of an educator will then evolve into designing such experiences and perhaps monitoring students' progress rather than standing in front of the classroom.

3) Systems engineer

Most experts in the field believe that the digital age is really just getting underway. In this context, there is an enormous demand for the people who can build, operate and protect the digital future.

Cybersecurity, machine learning and applying innovations like blockchain and AI are all specialties that will be in demand for years to come.

What is clear is that these technologies are moving ahead very quickly creating the need for engineers and engineering managers to stay current as newer and faster technologies become possible.

4) Marketeer

One task for marketing people is to figure out what products and services people really need and will pay for. Another is how to take new technologies and figure out how to make them relevant to solving people's problems. Targeted marketing based on studying people's online behavior is a growing field, although for many people it raises disturbing issues of privacy.

Marketing people, like everyone else, will need to keep learning and adapting to better tools with particular focus on the ability to sort through enormous amounts of data to discover patterns and insights.

5) Financial whiz

In most, if not all, human organization and certainly in business, somebody needs to keep track of the money. Capital needs to be raised, allocated, distributed and then measured both for the purpose of running the organization itself and in order to report to the relevant authorities, shareholders and other interested parties.

Automation and AI are changing some of the details of this function, but the essential *role* is future proof. A former student has, for example, launched a company that provides an AI which reads and processes invoices thus reducing the number of people needed in most firms by 80 percent. Someone, however, needs to set the policy about which supplier should be paid and how soon.

Finance, in many ways, is the language of business, and there will always be demand for people who are fully fluent in it.

6) Technician

As the world becomes more complex and automation takes over more and more of the physical world, there will be an ever-growing demand for technicians who can keep everything running. This will be particularly true as the world moves to a decentralized, low carbon energy mix and more and more devices are connected in what is called the the internet of things or IOT.

The way these jobs function will, however, evolve, and we should expect extensive use of augmented reality and AI in technical fields. Schneider Electric, for example, has a phone app that allows a technician to look at the inside of closed power cabinets that show the voltage across different circuits, the temperature running through the switches and other technical parameters.

One of the issues to bear in mind, however, is that in today's changing environment, technical positions may require constant retraining and education, and there may be a moment when entire job categories disappear due to technological advancement. Electric vehicles, for example, require less maintenance than cars that run on gasoline or diesel.

7) Salesperson

While it is clear that more and more goods and services are being bought and sold online, I suspect that there will always be demand for good salespeople in specific sectors both at the level of consumer salespeople and in the business-to-business space.

Business is often about trust and personal relationships, and the role of salespeople is to develop that trust. This is particularly true in certain parts of the world such as China where it is customary only to do business when a certain relationship or "Guanxi" is established.

People who can do this well will always be in demand, although the tools they use to know their customers and adapt their products and services will evolve very quickly.

8) Supply chain expert

Globalization has led many companies to source raw materials, subassemblies and finished products from all over the world. Apple, for example, sources most of its electronics and all of its phones from China and other countries in South East Asia.

Managing these global supply chains will be vital in the years ahead especially considering the potential changes in the geopolitical balance of the world as well as further advances in telecommunications, shipping and manufacturing technologies.

Advanced manufacturing actually may bring some production closer to markets as lot sizes go down and customized production becomes economically possible.

This *role* is also changing as consumers and regulators ask their companies to understand their sustainability footprint all the way down the supply chain, and many companies are rethinking the resilience of these global networks as a result of the disturbances caused by the pandemic and the invasion of Ukraine.

9) HR manager

Like many other *roles*, HR will evolve in the future but continue to be needed. When large firms think about the future, they often come to the conclusion that they will need significantly less people than they have today but also that they do not have many of the people they will need tomorrow.

This double challenge of reducing the workforce in light of automation but at the same time hiring the people to build and maintain the emerging business model will give HR a critical *role*.

Digitalization will also have a huge impact, but in the end of the day human judgment will be needed. LinkedIn, for example, can help connect recruiters and candidates, but it will be necessary to meet face to face or on screen (see Box 10).

10) Entrepreneur

With new challenges, technologies and increasingly complex work, the *role* of the entrepreneur is perhaps the most future proof of all. The challenge will be to make sure that the business model, base technologies and value proposition stay relevant as the world changes. This subject is discussed more deeply in Chapter 9.

Key Ideas Chapter 5

- Organizations are adapting the way they are set up and function in the post-pandemic world.
- It is better to think about *roles* and the value that they bring than job title or function.
- You may find that you will fit better with some *roles* more than others depending on the skills you have, what you are naturally suited for and the lifestyle you want to live.
- Some *roles* will continue to add value in the future including
    1. Health care and wellness practitioner,
    2. Educator,
    3. Systems engineer,
    4. Marketeer,
    5. Financial whiz,
    6. Technician,
    7. Salesperson,
    8. Supply chain expert,
    9. HR manager,
    10. Entrepreneur.

CHAPTER 6

PICKING A PLACE

The third part of thinking through what to do involves the issue of *place* or where to live and work. Where you are can be as important as what you do as different places offer us different things and also change over time.

The decision of where to be, and it is a decision, is important for a number of reasons. In the first place, the industrial fabric of a specific *place* is fairly stable over 10–20 years so that a certain *place* might be better than another in terms of working in a specific *space*.

Beyond the professional part of our lives, however, there are a number of aspects to living in different locations that we tend to lump under the idea of quality of life. This concept is a bit fuzzy and means different things to different people but is often associated with culture, climate, overall economic well-being, social and political issues and a range of topics including the quality of schools, level of crime and personal safety, and so on.

In this context, I feel it is important that you think through what quality of life means to you and your family, and this is discussed at some length below.

Another trend is that society is becoming more mobile so the whole idea of place is becoming a bit more nuanced as people commute shorter or longer distances, relocate to other parts of the world or find work which allows them to live virtually anywhere and digitally connect to their colleagues.

The pandemic has also weakened the connection between *place* and *space* that has existed up until now. I know many people who are currently working far from the place they would call their office. Many professional people have, for example, fled New York City in 2020 as a result of the pandemic and have been working remotely.

The other aspect of place that has been exposed by the pandemic is the differences between health care systems in different parts of the world. The United States, for example, has some of the best health care capabilities on the planet but has a highly decentralized system. Many European countries, on the other hand, have strong state-run health systems with a much smaller private sector.

Although this is not the place for a detailed discussion of which systems have done better during the crisis, health care quality, affordability and access are clearly issues to consider when looking at which place to live and work.

The Importance of Place

The importance of *place* is often underestimated. The English philosopher Roger Scruton[1] discusses the idea of love of home, or what he calls "oikophilia," to talk about people's attachment to a specific place. While living and working far from home can bring much satisfaction and growth, there are also enormous advantages to living close to family in a *place* where you feel you belong.

I myself have a hard time figuring out where I am from. I was born to American parents in London and then moved back to the United States when I was two years old. I grew up in the suburbs of New York and Boston and then went to boarding school in Massachusetts. I went to college in New York and Michigan and graduate school in Spain where I have lived for the last 30 years.

My parents were from New York City (Brooklyn) but left the city and raised us to believe that we could live anywhere and do anything we set our minds to. My mother moved to California after my father died when I was 16 so a reasonable question is where I am from?

Interestingly enough, my oldest daughter Alejandra has made her home in New York. Not long ago we were getting out of a taxi in the city and as I paid the driver and got out of the car, she told me that I "fit in" in the city.

Thinking about what she said it hit me that I do not really belong in Barcelona. I speak Spanish, for example, as opposed to the local language which is Catalan and do that with an American accent. Nobody really understands my sense of humor and my daughters have grown up accepting the fact that their dad is an expat.

In my last few trips to New York City I have spent time thinking through what Alejandra has told me and realized it is true. I feel at home in New York. I know where I am all the time and feel comfortable. I get the vibe and mood of the city and know how much to tip and what to say to the people I interact with.

---

1   R. Scruton, *How to Think Seriously about the Planet* (Oxford: Oxford University Press, 2012).

A friend who has been living in Rome for the last 20 years is from South Florida. As we happened to be in Miami at the same time we met for dinner, and I was amazed by how strong his sense of home was. Every time I see him in Europe he talks about moving back and maybe he will someday.

A Spanish friend who is a world class medical researcher and practitioner took more than a 60 percent cut in salary and a significant reduction in research money to come back to Spain to make sure that his daughters were able to be rooted in their own culture.

Do you know where you are from? Is there a *place* that has special importance to you and your family?

Richard Florida,[2] an American economist who lives in Toronto, talks about the importance of place and insists that where we live impacts, to a large degree, what we do, where we work, who our life partners are and what kind of future we can offer our children.

Many people I have spoken to over the years do choose the *place* they want to live as the first step in figuring out what to do precisely because of its importance.

Upon his retirement, my grandfather, Benjamin Rosenberg, moved to Jerusalem, and I will never forget how happy he was to finally be in a *place* where he could be himself among other people who also observed the Sabbath and where even the busses stopped running!

Clusters and Innovation Hubs

Over the years I have been approached by many professional people who wanted to relocate to Barcelona. Typically such people had been successful in a specific *space* and *role* back in their home country and were looking for a similar position which they imagined was waiting for them in the city.

What they typically did not think about was what that *space* really looked like in Barcelona? The city is strong on tourism, education and life sciences but weak in financial services and fast-moving consumer goods where there may be only one or two companies that could potentially hire such people.

Richard Florida argues that the growth of the global economy is largely taking place in about 50 major cities which are focused on one thing or another. These cities are also getting richer and richer and pulling away from the communities around them. He has found that people in such places have more to

---

2 R. Florida, *Who's Your City* (New York: Basic Books, 2008).

do with others in similar cities, wherever they are located, than with people in other communities in their own countries.

Probably the most famous and well-established example of a technological hub is the area just south of San Francisco commonly referred to as Silicon Valley. The history of the Valley goes back to Professor Frederick Terman, who taught Radio Science at Stanford in the 1920s and 1930s. Terman helped two of his students, Bill Hewitt and Dave Packard, to start their company. Since then generations of entrepreneurs have created thousands of companies leveraging a rich environment of potential partners and venture capitalists.

Enrico Moretti[3] goes deeper into the mechanism that is at work in such tech hubs. One critical part of their success is what he calls their "thick" labor markets meaning that there are many people in the area who have capabilities in a specific field.

By having many people available, companies choose to locate in the area to access this talent pool. Since there are so many companies, people interested in such work flock to such cities, and the two forces feed on each other in a positive cycle pushing these cities far beyond others in a specific technology or *space*.

Moretti finds that people in such hubs make more money than in other places because of the competition for talent. He also finds that all the people who live in such *places live better* than those in average towns and cities. This includes all of the teachers, police officers, plumbers, architects and even baristas at the coffee shops. The companies in the *space* pay top wages to those who can then afford to pay higher prices for services as well as local taxes.

The data shows differences in wealth but also in terms of health and life expectancy between people living in the emerging tech hubs and others in communities which have been left behind.

In the United States, places like Seattle, Austin, Boston and New York's Silicon Alley join Silicon Valley and San Francisco in leading the digital revolution, and other places are important in other fields such as biomedical research, aerospace, robotics, and so on.

Some industries, such as financial services, have been focused in certain places such as New York, London, Frankfurt and Tokyo, and if someone wants to "make it" in that field, they should think about moving there. The financial capital of Spain, for example, is in Madrid and the center for Europe, at least so far, has been London. I say so far because many leading financial institutions

---

3 E. Moretti, *The New Geography of Jobs* (Boston: Houghton Mifflin Harcourt, 2002).

have moved much of their staff from London to Frankfurt or Amsterdam as a result of the UK leaving the EU.

My guess is that although more and more people will work remotely, it will take a number of years before this connection fully fades away if it ever does. In any case, like the other two ideas *space* and *role*, it pays to look at the issue of *place* over time as our lives are long and things do evolve and change.

Do you know which cities have had the thickest labor markets for the *space* or *spaces* you are most interested in? The flip side of this logic is that if you really did want to live in a specific city or *place*, then think carefully about what the industrial fabric actually is and what *spaces* make sense to work in.

This will lead you to the question of whether you can wrap your head around working in that *space* and if you can find a *role* not only in which you will be happy but for which you can make a case that you would be able to add value.

Long-Distance Commuting, Business Travel and Expatriation

Many people live in one place and work in another. Typically this has involved driving or taking public transportation back and forth between work and home on a daily basis. Once travel time exceeds 30–45 minutes each way, it becomes significant and an important aspect of your overall quality of life.

In the postvirus world, it is likely that some people may choose to come to the workplace significantly less but perhaps would still want to come in for specific events and meetings perhaps a couple of days per week. Others will not have a choice due to the nature of their work or the attitude their employers take once the world gets to some level of normal.

I know many people with extremely long commutes who, even before the pandemic, would stay a night or two "in town" or work from home a day or two a week. Both solutions make sense from a travel perspective but can impact family life and work depending on the situation.

At home, being away on a regular basis can strain relationships and create unforeseen problems with your spouse, children or other people who are important to you. At work, being out a couple of days a week can also cut you out of important informal communication and also be perceived as unfair by colleagues who do not or cannot enjoy such flexibility.

The combination of air travel and telecommunications platforms such as Zoom and Teams makes it possible to go even further than the classical commute and actually live and work in different cities, time zones or even countries. Such arrangements are certainly possible and increasingly frequent especially after our collective experience during 2020. There are, however, important personal and professional issues to consider.

I have personally commuted long distances to work and underestimated the strain that I placed on my family. In my late 30s I was averaging four to eight flights a week and sometimes those were transatlantic.

Flying out on Monday morning (or even Sunday night), meeting with people in a number of places and getting back home on Thursday or Friday was normal for me as it has been for tens of thousands of managers. The logic was that human contact was key to building trust, and there was no substitute for "being there."

Some years ago, I found myself flying to Shanghai from Barcelona to have lunch with a group of program participants, and if that's not crazy then what is? The reason for the quick trip to China is typical of the logic that prevailed in business for many years.

My school had a joint program with the China Europe International Business. It was considered polite to personally meet them and give them a formal welcome before they came to Barcelona for the next part of their course. Since neither the dean nor the associate dean were available, I had to go and fly straight back for another class.

My guess is that we will see this type of travel drop off over the next few years as the pandemic has taught the international business community that it is not necessary. People will still travel for business but most of us have become quite proficient on having all kinds of meetings and events in a virtual format.

Unlike long-distance business travel, my guess is that relocation will continue to be an important aspect of the modern business world. As a manager gains experience in an organization, it often makes sense both for themselves and the company to give them bigger and bigger challenges. Often those challenges are in a different location, city or even another country. Many large firms routinely rotate people from place to place in an effort to create more "rounded" managers.

At some companies, such as the Ford Motor Company, this idea is deeply embedded in the culture, and an assignment usually lasts about three years. While such practices have a number of very positive professional benefits for all concerned, they can be challenging to families in general and to the partner of the manager being asked to go far away.

In today's increasingly globalized business environment such assignments are also getting farther and farther away from home, and while a transfer from one side of a country to another is one thing, going to a completely new country or even another part of the world is another. Such experiences can be very rewarding for the whole family but must be made carefully.

The biggest problem is sometimes getting back especially for people coming from relatively small countries or cities. Typically, a young man or woman is promoted in their home country until there is really nowhere else to go. If they are "lucky" then someone will give them a chance to move to a larger country, market or plant where they can do the same thing in a larger context.

This process will repeat itself, perhaps with some deliberate job rotation, until they get to the head office in a critical regional function. Often there is no job in their home market that is big enough for them.

There are no easy answers to make choices about international schools, dual careers and a number of other issues you will have to face if you pursue an international career.

What I do recommend is to try to think through the implications of the different choices you make and weigh both the positives and negatives as well as you can. I also recommend carefully evaluating your family's appetite for adventure on the one hand and risk on the other.

Telecommuting

One solution to the issue about where to live and work is to telecommute. There are an increasingly large number of professions and even companies that take advantage of digital technology and telecommunications to make where we live virtually independent of where we work. Many editors, designers, coders, and so on, never go to the office in the classic sense. This trend has, of course, accelerated as a result of the pandemic.

Automatic, for example, the company that publishes WordPress, has always had an almost completely virtual workforce. WordPress is the leading application to build and update web pages and is what I use, for example, to publish my blog.

Automatic's headquarters are in San Francisco but very few people work there. Back in 2011, I had the pleasure of attending one of their periodic town hall meetings in which the CEO spoke with the entire company to explain how things were going and get their input.

I remember about 50–100 people standing in a large open space but was told that some thousands more were tuning into the event online. There were even a couple of remotely controlled robots moving around with live video feeds of remote attendees interacting with people face to face during the meeting!

The company's attitude is that they want the best people they can get for every specific task, and they simply do not care where they live. Coordination is maintained by a system of chats and logs which essentially record all ongoing conversations about new products and changes to the software.

Another layer to this discussion has to do with freelancers and other professionals involved in the gig economy. The pros and cons of working this way are explored in Chapter 10.

In another example a former student lives in Barcelona but has started up a block chain company in Singapore. He explained to me that the technical team and its head are in Chiang Mai in Thailand because that was where he could recruit the people he needed on a freelance basis to build the algorithm.

In some cases, the *role* in question does require a physical presence but can be managed in short time periods between which the professional lives in a place that they have chosen.

A former colleague, for example, lives near the beach in Thailand but has been teaching at schools in Shanghai, New York and London. Some of his teaching schedule, like my own, has of course moved online.

Telecommuters, however, sometimes may not have the same level of social connection to their colleagues as people who work together every day. Also, for many people, work is a social activity and not all of us have the discipline, space available or family situation required to work productively from home.

One solution to this problem is the idea of shared office space which has become very popular in many of the technological hubs around the world. Such spaces offer desks or small offices but also connections to other people, conference facilities, technological assets and other perks so that it is possible to work more or less on your own but still go to work every day and mix with other people.

The future of telecommuting, shared office space and many other basic assumptions about the world of work are in flux as a result of the measures put in place to control the spread of the pandemic and the way companies and managers have responded to those measures.

In the future perhaps you will be able to completely separate the *place* you live from the *place* you work. I do think that this process will take 5–10 years to play out depending of course on the *role* you choose to play and the *space* and even company that you choose to play it in.

The Future of a Place

When you move to a city or region you are also making a statement about your thoughts about its economic, environmental and geopolitical future whether you do so implicitly or explicitly. A move to Moscow or Kiev, for example, made the implicit assumption that war was unlikely despite the tension in the region.

Perhaps the first issue which one should think about is the likely economic future of a given *place* given its role in the regional and global economy. Most economists agree that the next 20 years will see the continuing rise of China and other Asian countries as a percentage of the overall global economy and the mega cities of Asia will clearly be sources of economic growth.

Other places will continue to be the focus for innovation and growth in specific *spaces*. Living in such innovation hubs offers significant advantages in terms of job prospects and income potential, and part of the challenge is to figure out which of those cities and technologies will be important over time.

Richard Florida points out, for example, that in 1990 Detroit was far ahead of Seattle but that 25 years later, the fortunes of the two cities changed in line with the fates of the large American automotive companies on the one hand and Microsoft and other companies in the software *space*, which are located nearby, on the other.

The second issue has to do with the overall quality of life including the prevalence of crime, traffic patterns, the quality of schools, arts and cultural activities. These aspects also change over time. Probably the best thing to do is to look at the trends. If the schools in a given location have been getting better over the last five to ten years, then it is likely that they will continue to do so. New York City's crime rate, for example, peaked in 1990 and then started a 30-year decline making the city one of the safest in the United States today.

The third issue is a *places*'s natural environment including the presence of green spaces, the condition of air and water and access to high-quality food. Shanghai, for example, is a fast-growing, exciting place to live and work and will clearly be one of the most dynamic cities for many years to come. There are, on the other hand, serious concerns about the city's air quality, water purity and food safety. The outbreak of COVID-19 in China raised further doubts about Shanghai even though Wuhan is hundreds of miles up the river.

On the other side of the scale is Boulder, Colorado, which is relatively small, has excellent air quality and is surrounded by parkland called the green belt that is public land and will, in theory, never be developed.

From Boulder it is a short drive to the majestic Rocky Mountains, and if that is your passion, there may be no better *place* which is still only an hour from a major airport and a major city.

A related issue is the exposure that different places have to climate change. On this issue I would stress not only long-term questions about temperature and desertification, which can be significant over the next 20–30 years, but much more immediate concerns such as hurricanes and typhoons and the storm surges that come with them.

The last issue I suggest you to think about is the geopolitical stability of a *place*, especially if you are looking at countries which have or will be undergoing profound political change or are in some of the key hot spots around the world discussed in Chapter 1.

Years ago a man came to see me who had been working in a developing country which went through a rebel uprising which led to a brutal civil war. After seeing bodies in the street on the way to school, his wife took the kids back to Europe and gave him the ultimatum of finding a job back home or ending their marriage.

Place is more important than *space* or *role* when thinking beyond your professional aspirations to include all of the other aspects of our life such as family, friends and the way you choose to spend time when you are not working.

In my experience this idea of thinking about the future of a given *place* is normally not given enough weight in people's thought process. Thinking about such issues and including them in the scenarios you develop is your responsibility and will help you to find the right combination.

The next chapter will go into more detail on how to do that.

Key Ideas Chapter 6

- The *place* you live is perhaps even more important than the *role* you play or the *space* you work in considering the overall quality of life.
- There has been a relationship between *place* and *space* as certain activities are increasingly concentrating in specific places or technology hubs.
- As a result of the global pandemic, some assumptions about the nature of work and its relationship to place are changing, although it is hard to know how fast things will change and will such changes be permanent.
- Commuting, business travel, relocation and telecommuting all bring important trade-offs which need to be considered.

- In thinking about *place*, you ought to think about how the place will evolve over time as well as your own needs and interests will also change.
- The natural environment and geo-political situation also change the nature of a *place*.

BOX 6: FRAGILE STATES

In 1995, the Fund for peace teamed up with *Foreign Policy* to publish a ranking of all the countries in the world in terms of how stable and functioning their government is. The ranking was called the "Failed State Index" up to 2014 when the name was changed to the "Fragile State Index."

The analysis is based on looking at twelve different indicators of stability grouped into four categories which are the country's overall cohesion, its economic trajectory, political situation, social indicators and if other countries are deeply involved in country's politics, security situation or economy.

Cohesion indicators include the security apparatus and its ability to combat terrorism, organized crime, etc.; the degree to which the elite of the country is divided into factions along ethnic, class or racial lines; and the presence of important divisions in civil society such as ethnic or religious strife.

Economic indicators include overall economic progress or its lack including the percentage of the population living in poverty, the level of inequality in the country, and the degree to which both poor and rich people move away causing a humanitarian crisis on the one hand and a brain drain on the other.

In political terms, the index looks at the overall degree to which the sate represents the will of the people, the quality of its public services and respect for human rights and the rule of law.

The social indicators are the overall demographic pressure and if there are large numbers of refugees or other displaced people in relation to the overall population.

According to the 2021 analysis, the five most fragile countries in the world are Yemen, Somalia, South Sudan, Syria and the Democratic Republic of Congo. On the other end of the spectrum, the five most stable and functioning countries are nations of Finland, Norway, Switzerland, Denmark and Iceland. You can find a specific country at https://fragilestatesindex.org/ or look at this year's map below.

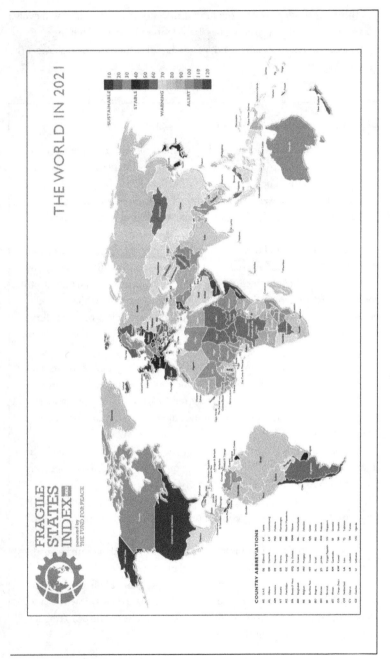

CHAPTER 7

FINDING THE RIGHT COMBINATION

The global pandemic and the war in Europe has caused many people to question their basic assumptions about what is really important and the value they place on their health and relationships with family and friends. It has also called into question some symbols of wealth, while at the same time, underlining the importance of having sufficient living space, some savings in the bank and good access to Wi-Fi.

The core idea of this book is that in this complex world, you can find a combination of *space*, *role* and *place* that will allow you to connect with things you are passionate about, do tasks that you are or can become good at and live in a city or town that is right for you. By finding the right balance between paid work and everything else you do in your life, it should be possible to be happy. This chapter explores different aspects of putting together the three ideas of *space*, *role* and *place*.

There is, to start with, an entire field of research into what makes people happy. My former colleague, Manel Baucells, and his coauthor Rakish Sarin say that we can engineer happiness and that it is about matching expectations to reality.

In terms of material wealth, an important issue is how much is enough to pay for the life we need and want. A different but related issue has to do with how much we ought to save either for potential emergencies or to finance the last phase of our lives when we may not choose to or be able to continue to work at the same rhythm or make the same kind of money.

There are trade-offs to consider and finding balance is key. Very high-paying jobs in banking, for example, require tremendous amounts of time and dedication as well as strong finance skills and an outstanding ability to manage complex client relationships. A hard look at our commitments to family, friends and ourselves is one of the most important issues to consider.

A final issue discussed in this chapter is the source of satisfaction at work. On that topic Daniel Pink makes the case that professional people are not really motivated by money as long as they do not feel underpaid. For him what gives us job satisfaction are the concepts of mastery, autonomy and a sense of purpose.

Mastery has to do with the fact that we tend to enjoy doing what we are good at. Autonomy is the degree to which we feel that we control our own destiny. A sense of purpose, which is explored in more depth in Chapter 11, gets at the heart of why we do what we do and what it means to us.

Loneliness, Despair and Gratitude

Aside from the obvious impact of illness and death, the pandemic which began in early 2020 and rapidly spread around the world had an enormous impact on other aspects of people's well-being.

Hundreds of millions of people in countries around the world have experienced anxiety about the virus as well as concerns about making ends meet. Cut off from friends and family during lockdowns, many people also experienced extreme loneliness and depression.

In a study by the Brookings Institution,[1] rates of overdoses of opiates, suicide and other deaths of despair, as sociologists call the problem, sharply increased as a result of the pandemic. The study also points out how these trends were far more pronounced in poor and lower middle income people than the rich in the United States and around the world.

For many people the pandemic was a very stressful experience as a result of trying to balance work and children. Stress also affects our physical well being which was made worse in lock down because many gyms and other leisure activities were closed.

For some, however, the pandemic also offered a respite from business travel, commuting and other annoyances which are common to modern life. Many people I know found enormous pleasure in sitting down with their families for breakfast, lunch and dinner during confinement.

Others found the experience incredibly lonely when they were literally cut off from their wider network of friends and family. Video and telephone calls

---

1 C. Graham and L. Pasvolsky, "The Human Costs of the Pandemic: Is It Time to Prioritize Well-Being?" in *Reimagining the Global Economy: Building Back Better in Post Covid-19 World* (The Brooking Institution, 2020), pp. 79–85.

could make up for some of the lost connection but for many people this was far from enough.

These restrictions also hit older people very hard as many of them could not go on their regular walks and shopping as they were particularly felt to be at risk for COVID-19. Losing a year and a half is tough for anyone but perhaps even harder for older retirees.

Perhaps the most important aspect was that the situation forced many people to recognize what is most important to us and to be grateful for what we do have.

What Makes People Happy

In *Engineering Happiness*,[2] Manel Baucells and Rakesh Sarin make the case that it is possible to quantify happiness and work out its fundamental laws.

Their work is based on psychological research from around the world and seems to apply to all types of people. I find it particularly relevant after the pandemic.

Baucells and Sarin postulate their six laws of happiness as follows:

The first and most important is that the happiness we receive from an experience or an object we get is equal to the reality of that experience minus the expectations we had for it. If our hopes are too high, we will be disappointed no matter how objectively good the experience is.

Both experiences and objects can make us happier. The only difference is that we pay for objects with money and experiences with our time. Baucells and Sarin do make a distinction between things that always give us the same pleasure, that they call basic goods, as opposed to others in which the happiness we receive changes that they call adaptive goods.

Basic goods include eating enjoyable food, spending time with our partner and family and perhaps listening to great music as these activities will almost always make us happy. Adaptive goods include bigger houses, more luxurious cars or cell phones with more features.

The second law is that of changing expectations. As we surround ourselves with nicer things, we tend to want even more creating an endless race between reality and expectations. Our expectations are also driven by comparing

---

2 Manel Baucells and Rakesh Sarin, *Engineering Happiness: A New Approach for Building a Joyful Life*. 1st ed. (Berkeley; Los Angeles; London: University of California Press, 2012).

ourselves and our experience to that of other people. Baucells and Sarin refer to conspicuous goods which are things we tend to compare. One important way to ensure your happiness is to compare yourself with the right group of people.

I know, for example, many people who feel they are underpaid but make much more money than their parents ever dreamed of. They compare themselves to their neighbors or peers rather than where they came from. People from wealthy families sometimes have the opposite problem as they compare themselves with their family rather than their peers.

The third law of happiness is that humans have a harder time with loss than with gain so that we are more unhappy if we lose something than happy if we received the same thing.

The fourth law is about how the more we have of something the less it makes us happy. The fifth is that in some cases we get satiated or full. Even our favorite food may not make us happy if we have just finished lunch.

The final law of happiness is that we tend to give more importance to momentary happiness than what we know will make us happy in the long run.

While there is much more to the model of happiness, such as the difference between peak periods of joy or pain and the way our memory processes such data, the reason for exploring the model is to encourage you to take a careful stock of what really makes you happy as you start to explore different combinations of *space*, *role* and *place*.

The basic idea is to figure out a career path in which you can make enough money to fulfill your dreams and ambitions while still finding time for friends and family. All this depends on your personal situation and will change over time (see Box 7).

BOX 7: CHANGING IDEAS OF WHAT MAKES US HAPPY

Two professors at the London Business School, Lynda Gratton and Andrew Scott have written about the professional implications of our living longer in their book *A Hundred Year Life*.[3]

The book argues that as people live longer and longer, the idea of one profession for 30–40 years is no longer viable, and we will most likely have

---

3 L. Gratton and A. Scott, *The Hundred Year Life* (London: Bloomsbury, 2016).

a series of different professional phases in our lives as we grow older and enter into a long-term relationship, have or adopt children, and so on.

This idea of professional phases will be developed more fully in Chapter 10, but it is worth mentioning here as what makes you happy is likely to change as you go through life.

If you are single and just out of school, you may find that sports, travel, experience and meeting new people are the kinds of things that make you happy.

If you decide to share your life with someone else, then figuring out what makes you happy is a little more complicated. This gets even harder if and when children come into the picture although for some it actually makes things clearer.

For many people, the first baby is often seen as an added part of an adventure and can be compatible with many of the interests and activities that people had before having the child. The second baby makes things harder and I have seen many people give up some of their passions in order to spend more time with their immediate family or even relocate back home to have deeper contact with their extended family.

Later in life there are also changing circumstances, and Gratton and Scott write extensively about a specific phase in life prior to retirement, in the classic sense, but perhaps after a person's professional prime when making money is no longer the primary objective.

The point is that happiness is different at each of these different phases and I urge you to reflect on what is most important to you today and perhaps over the next 5–10 years again depending on where you are on life's journey.

Wants and Needs

When engineers embark on a new car design they look at two types of features that the new car should have. Wants are the features that it would be nice to have and needs are that are absolutely essential for the new car to be able to compete in the marketplace.

Applying the same construct to your life you should be able to distinguish between items such as housing, health care and other living expenses on the one hand and the nice to haves such as holidays and sports clubs on the other. You may have found that you learned to live without things during the pandemic that you thought were essential.

In my own story I took a massive pay cut when I chose to join the faculty of a business school and give up my job as a partner in an international executive search firm. I was able to do that because I had the support of my spouse who was trying to get me to tune into things which were more important and insisted that we did not need the (extra) money.

I suggest you try to determine what part of the money you and your family spend is really needed and what part is "extra." One can, of course, reduce expectations on the one hand or find a way to make more money on the other. Using Baucells and Sarin's model, however, making more money may become an endless race between reality and expectations.

Financial security is important, and understanding what it means for you involves looking at monthly and annual expenses and articulating clearly the difference between our wants and needs in six essential areas as follows:

Housing

According to the Bureau of Labor Statistics,[4] housing is the number one cost for American consumers and represents about a third of their total spending. The exact percentage depends on whether they are married, are single or have children. Surprisingly, people in bigger households spend a little bit less on housing as a percentage than singles.

Part of the story is how much housing costs in different places. New York and London are clearly much more expensive than Jackson, Mississippi or Zaragoza, a medium sized city in Spain. A second part of the question is how much housing costs relative to the salaries that are typically paid in these locations. As a percent of average salary, Beijing turns out to be much more expensive than New York City.

A third issue is what kind of housing makes sense to you and your family. In many parts of the world, for example, a detached one family house in a safe place is only available in very exclusive neighborhoods which are very expensive. Other places offer better schools, access to nature and cleaner air and water.

The last point is the difference between the cost of renting a place to live and the total cost of home ownership given the interest rates around the world. This calculation is different in different places, but in general terms an efficient

---

4 https://www.bls.gov/news.release/cesan.nr0.htm, accessed October 2019.

housing market, like that in the United States, tends to make rents track closely the financial cost of owning a similar house or condo.

Transportation

Transportation is the second biggest expense and on average represents 16 percent of expenditures in the United States.[5] Besides the trade-off between private and public transportation, there is a major trend in the world today which appears to be moving from car ownership to mobility or having access to transportation when you need it. Concerns about the pandemic have caused this trend to stall but my guess is it will come back.

There are a number of companies exploring new business models which allow you to have access to the car you need when you need it for a flat monthly fee, and all the large carmakers are working on different approaches.

Another approach is to take advantage of ride-sharing and a variety of transportation companies like Uber and Lift. Depending on the how you need to go from place to place, it may make more sense not to own a car and use a combination of other types of services including using the small electric scooters that have become popular in many towns and cities.

Health care

Health care and health insurance are large items particularly in the United States which has no national health coverage unlike many countries around the world such Canada, the UK, Germany and Spain.

In the United States, Americans spent $11,582 per person in 2019 which added up to $3.8 trillion or just under 18 percent of the entire economy. It is the highest in the world. The total cost for 2020 and 2021 will be even higher as a result of the virus. Millions of people in the United States have actually lost their health insurance due to the economic contraction and even those with insurance may face enormous costs if they or a loved one is hospitalized.

The purpose of this discussion is not to enter into the political debate concerning health care but to stress the importance of having coverage in case of catastrophic illness if you live in the United States or in another country where you cannot rely on the public system for one reason or another.

---

5 https://www.bls.gov/news.release/cesan.nr0.htm, accessed October 2019.

Day-to-day living expenses

In addition to these big ticket items you need to account for a host of day-to-day expenses such as food, clothes, utilities, and schools. The amount needed for such things depends on our choices about where to live as these costs tend to track housing and are much higher in some places than others.

In addition to location, our choices also drive the budget we need. Organic food, for example, usually comes at a premium price and meat costs more than vegetables.

Schooling is a complex subject and again depends on where you live. In the United States, public schools are managed by local school boards and financed through property taxes so that expensive housing often brings high-quality public schools as part of the package. Many people opt for private education for a variety of reasons, and there is a growing movement toward home schooling in certain parts of the country.

Nice to haves

While there is no clear rule between wants and needs which can be applied to everyone, in your life, it should be possible to separate the day-to-day living expenses from things that would be nice to have.

You may, for example, consider the latest smartphone and an unlimited data contract as absolutely essential while someone else might think it is clearly a luxury. Your need for other electronics, expensive cars or vacation homes depend on who you are.

What I suggest is that you spend some time thinking about what you really need and what is clearly optional. Going back to the idea of engineering happiness, Baucells and Sarin recommend gradually working up to higher levels of goods and experiences over the course of our lives so that we find satisfaction in every step along the journey.

Savings

The crisis caught many people with little-to-no savings. As a result, many governments around the world put rules in place to limit home evictions but many people have lost their homes anyway.

This chapter would not be complete without some thoughts on financial planning. In my experience, money does not buy happiness at any time, particular later in life, but its absence can cause insecurity, distress and worse.

According to the head of the consulting business that I worked in back in the 1980s, a good plan should be to use the first 20 years of our professional life to buy a house, the next 10 or so to pay for the children's education and then the last 10 to prepare for retirement. The model is pretty simple but was effective for many people in the past.

A problem with that model, however, is that people all over the world tend to live longer and enjoy a much more active life through their 70s and 80s, if not beyond.

One of the key questions to consider in this context is, how much is enough for you? The objective of the discussion is not to summarize the field of financial planning or paraphrase books such as Lee Eisenberg's *The Number* but to add a placeholder to the discussion so we can factor in savings into the overall equation.

Of course, all of this depends on who you are as well as where and how you choose to live. Upon her official retirement my mother bought herself a nice, four-room house with a garden in her favorite town and lives happily on her pension plus the money she makes from her limited investments. For at least 10 years, she also worked in different short-term jobs and even now sits on a number of committees in her community. She is 87.

Another friend divides his time between playing golf, working on the board of a local nonprofit and learning Chinese. Part of the reason he has plenty of money is that he still lives in the same house his kids grew up in and has no expensive tastes.

Each of us has to think through this question and consider some of the real possibilities that might emerge in our life span and what kind of a life we want to live.

Finding Balance

Perhaps the most difficult issue is to find balance between our personal and professional life and also between our aspirations and what we actually choose to do.

What took me a long time to understand is the tremendous toll that certain jobs like my own career as a consultant places on personal life. The biggest problem is that if you get involved in a high powered career and are good at it, you may come to enjoy it.

Flying from place to place, doing interesting things and making good money is not only fun but also addictive. If most of the people you work with do the same thing, then you begin to think that it's normal and forget that most people actually go home every day after work and some actually go home for lunch!

HR people often talk about work–life balance, but in my experience, a lot of the best jobs simply do not tolerate one! If we look at the list of *roles* presented in Chapter 5, each one has a different implication about work–life balance.

1) Educator

One advantage of teaching or working in an educational institution is you get summers and holidays off, and this is true today whether you are teaching six year olds or MBAs at one of the world's top business schools. The downside is that you can basically never miss class, and depending on the place you teach and the level, you may have to do other things like meet with parents, play a role in school administration, do scientific research or write books.

All of this takes time and energy and to do it at the highest level takes a lot of it. The good news is that you can generally choose where to focus that energy and write what you want to write or coach the sports team that is close to your passion.

As most teachers have learned in during the pandemic, online teaching can be more invasive but also offers flexibility in terms of location which can be a positive trade-off.

2) Systems Engineer

People involved in building our digital future do it all the time. In fact many of the companies in this *space* offer amazing benefits such as free food at all hours of the day and night, concierge services including laundry and even allow you to bring your dog to work. The idea was that the people who work in these firms should never have to leave the building. For many such people they would not want to anyway.

Although virtual companies like Automatic, mentioned above, used to be the exception, the pandemic has caused many of these companies and the people who work in them to rethink the idea of working remotely.

Regardless of whether they are working on site or at home, my experience is that the architects of the digital future work very long hours and are deeply immersed in what they do. While you might see this as a good thing, it can cause strain on relationships particularly if the other people in your life do not share the same passion.

3) Marketeer

Marketing people do have something of a work–life balance as their work typically does finish at a reasonable hour, but they often love what they do and continue to work and read in to the evenings.

They also have a rhythm to their professional life depending on the particular *space* as there are certain times of year when sales are at their highest, budgets are due, or everyone goes off to an international trade show.

4) Financial whiz

Depending on the specific *role* they play, finance people are always busy at the end of the month or year. Those that work in the investment banks, private equity firms, venture capitalists and at the very top of a large corporate's mergers and acquisitions teams work even harder, especially when a deal is on.

In theory, the rewards of this kind of work can be astronomical, but the cost is high. People who work 70–80 hours a week basically have no time for anything else. They arrive home when their spouse and children, if they are lucky enough to have them, are asleep and may not even see them on many weekends.

Many of my students have, over the years, pursued this option with the idea that they will get out at some point in the future. What they don't realize is that the life at the top of the global financial markets will change them, and it may not be so easy to stop.

Part of that change involves the process of adapting their expectations to every higher level of compensation and rewards. The other has to do with genuinely enjoying the rush and adrenaline of working on the deal.

5) Technician

Technical people generally lead more balanced lives than managers and get home after a long day's work. Highly specialized technicians, however, do need to be ready to travel far from home for significant periods of time. Such jobs, however, do tend to pay well so again it is all about trade-offs and balance.

Pilots, flight attendants, officers on merchant ships and the crews of oil rigs, for example, normally work on a rotating basis where they are away for days, weeks or even months at a time but then have significant time off to enjoy family or pursue other interests.

Such a schedule has a huge upside but also a downside as your rotation may coincide with a child's birthday or some other important event. On a deeper level, it is hard for some people to go back and forth between being on and off. Partners and families will also have to adapt to having someone who is either missing from the family's day-to-day life or always around.

6) Salesperson

Historically, salespeople travel a lot. If that travel is local or regional, then they can get home on a regular basis. As they get promoted, however, the geographic scope tends to increase making trips longer or farther away.

Perhaps the most punishing role I know of these days is to have sales responsibility for what many companies call the Asia Pacific region. Roles like this require constant travel since the key markets are far away from eachother and require 6–12 hour long plane rides in order to visit face to face.

The one thing salespeople need is a genuine interest in building up long-term client relationships as this is still a critical aspect of the *role* and requires, like everything else, time and energy.

Although much sales activity has moved online as a result of the pandemic, my guess is that face-to-face interaction will still be required to develop long-term relationships. Looking ahead salespeople may travel less than they did before but will still travel more than people in other *roles*.

7) Supply chain expert

The advantage of being in supply chain management as opposed to sales is that typically the sellers come to you rather than the other way around. This potentially means that business travel could be much less than for the salespeople.

Executives with an international responsibility, however, do need to get out and visit their suppliers, and increasingly companies are dictating increased sustainability performance from their supply base with needs to be checked periodically.

If everything is working properly then supply chain executives may have a predictable life. Unfortunately, things do happen and they might happen more frequently in the future due to geopolitical change and extreme weather caused by climate change. What this means is that people in this business may normally get home at night but will often have to deal with crises as they come up, whatever it takes.

8) Health care and wellness practitioner

Outside of the 24/7 period that many doctors go through during their residency or fellowship training, the health care profession has normally offered some balance as people tend to stay local and work long but reasonable hours.

This thinking went out the window as the virus peaked in different cities and regions around the world pushing the health care system and the people who worked in it to and past the limit.

Time, of course, is only one issue. Health care professionals also deal with people in difficult conditions and often suffer extreme stress as their work carries enormous responsibility.

Added to this is the real and present danger of working in health care during an infectious epidemic. According to a study undertaken by *The Guardian* and Kaiser Health, 2,900 health care workers died in the Unites States as a result of the pandemic in 2020 alone. In addition to the prospect of getting sick is the physical and emotional burden of taking precautions and worrying about the possibility.

EMTs and emergency room personnel work not only night shifts but also under enormous pressure, which can literally mean life or death for their patients.

All of this needs to be balanced against the satisfaction that people in these professions get from helping people. In my experience, doctors, nurses, chiropractors, physical therapists and all of the support and administrative people who work in health care get tremendous satisfaction from doing something they feel is important.

9) HR manager

In terms of work–life balance, the *role* of HR manager will be positive until they begin to cover larger and larger geographies. Unlike salesmen who always travel from place to place, HR managers will only start to travel as they take on specific assignments such as global recruiting manager or international compensation and benefits director.

One thing HR managers do need to deal with are problems in life and work, which sometimes overlap with each other. While hiring new personnel can be rewarding, there are moments when HR has to fire individuals or large numbers of people.

Like health care workers, it is necessary to have some degree of clinical detachment to ensure that you can do your job to the highest ethical and professional standards without allowing it to affect your personal life.

10) Entrepreneur

Depending on the nature of the company, an entrepreneur may be able to create a sensible work–life balance in terms of the hours they are at the office or the company. What they normally have a very difficult time doing, however, is to completely disconnect, and this can be exhausting for the entrepreneur and frustrating for their friends and family.

Although this idea will be explored further in a section in Chapter 9, my advice is always to build companies which are close to your passion so that if you do end up working all the time, at least you will do what you really love.

Motivations

In his book, *Drive*, Daniel Pink does an outstanding job of synthesizing a large body of research to get at how people in professional *roles* are motivated. His basic insight is that professional people are not really motivated by money as long as they do not feel underpaid. For Pink, these things can largely be reduced to autonomy, mastery and a sense of purpose.

Mastery has to do with the fact that we tend to enjoy doing what we are good at. People learn to play musical instruments, sail, fly planes, and so on, and get tremendous pleasure from improving their skill. In *Outliers*,[6] Malcolm Gladwell popularized the idea that it takes 10,000 hours to master anything.

This is related to work done by Marcus Buckingham and his series of books on the topic of strengths. What Buckingham found is that people tend to be happy and productive at work when they spend most of their time doing things they are good at.

Autonomy is the degree to which we feel that we control our own destiny. This is part of the insight behind the agile form of organization that is currently becoming more common and is also connected to empowerment.

---

6 M. Gladwell, *Outliers: The Story of Success, Little, Brown and Company* (2008).

Essentially humans like to take responsibility for aspects of their work environment and are demotivated when simply told what to do.

Pink's final motivational factor is having a sense of purpose and being able to connect our own sense of what is important in the world to the purpose of the organization in which we work.

Pink's framework may be helpful in looking at different combinations of *space*, *role* and *place*. You might, for example, be looking at a relatively safe opportunity where you can continue in a *role* you know well which pays well in a *space* that is familiar, although perhaps not so meaningful.

By combining this analysis with a look at financial rewards, impact on family and other factors such as professional risk and the exposure to global trends, an overall rating can be worked out to compare very different options.

The framework might be helpful to choose between specific opportunities or companies as the nature of an organization's culture will largely determine the autonomy people have.

It is possible to develop the combinations starting with *space*, *role* or *place*, although in the end, they need to make sense as a whole. Compromise may be required as it may be hard to find the ideal combination of *space* and *role*, which happens to be in the right *place* and be able to generate enough money to make everything work out.

Once several combinations have been selected, the next part of the process is to figure out how to get there. In some cases, this will mean changing jobs within the context of a specific phase in our professional life. In others, it might mean making a more abrupt break and embarking on a new phase all together. One way of understanding this is that we will have a number of such combinations in the course of our life and that they will fall into a few broad phases.

Chapter 8 drills down into a number of the issues associated with changing jobs, while Chapter 9 then goes onto the question of making more fundamental choices such as moving from one phase to another.

Key Ideas Chapter 7

- The global pandemic has caused illness, death, loneliness and despair, while at the same time, reminding many of us what is most important.
- Your happiness is a function of the reality of your life compared to your expectations from it.
- We can distinguish between the things we need in our lives and those that we want.

- Money has a role in helping us achieve our aims but perhaps does not lead to happiness on its own.
- Different *roles* come with built-in trade-offs in terms of time to pursue one's interests outside of work as well as stress levels and even physical danger.
- Daniel Pink offers the ideas of mastery, autonomy and a sense of purpose as the best way to evaluate if you will be motivated by a specific combination of *role, place* and *space.*

CHAPTER 8

CHANGING JOBS

Whether you have been fired, laid off, are trying to decide whether to leave your current position or are graduating from school, getting a new job can be stressful.

In addition to the emotional and financial stress that you are probably under, you might find that you are facing a deeper question which is whether to find a new job as soon as possible or take advantage of the situation to rethink your career goals. Having gone through this a few times myself, I have come to the conviction that such changes are tremendous opportunities for personal growth. While seeing the bright side is very difficult, I urge you to be open to the idea that things will work out for the best.

If you are one of the millions of people affected by the economic impact of the pandemic, it may be particularly difficult to be optimistic because the situation has called into question the very survival of certain *roles* and *spaces*.

Part of the story is that 2021 has seen shortages of labor in a number of specific *roles*, *spaces* and *places* as parts of the global economy has come back faster than anticipated. This creates an additional question as to whether you should take the first reasonable job that comes along or hold out for something which either pays better or is closer to your heart.

Here I make a distinction between getting a new job within a phase of our professional life and moving from phase to phase. Phases are periods of 10–20 years in which you will likely work in a series of related jobs.

This chapter is about getting a new job and Chapter 10 will deal with changing from phase to phase. I will start by discussing losing a job and then move on to a different topic which is deciding if it is time to leave your current position.

I will also go into the value that executive search and selection companies can bring to you as well as placement agencies which operate from a different perspective.

The chapter closes with crafting your CV and cover letter, interviewing and conducting salary negotiations.

Losing a Job

Getting fired or laid off is a traumatic experience, and there is no point in pretending that it is not.

The first time it happened to me was in 1985. I was an engineer working for a company in Houston that built and managed offshore oil drilling platforms, and my most recent assignment was a construction project in Japan. The price of oil had dropped from $28 per barrel to $8 in the spring of 1985, and by late July the company decided to lay off 20 percent of its engineering team. Upon returning to Houston, I was told that I was part of the 20 percent, given a very small check and sent to an outplacement class.

They say that everything happens for a reason, and I know now that I would never have been an outstanding engineer. Getting laid off led me to come to Spain, do my MBA and meet the mother of my children.

Who to blame?

While I know how painful such a situation can be, it is essential that you reflect upon the reasons that have caused the situation. Did you lose your job, for example, due to the pandemic and resulting economic situation? Was it some other issue facing the industry or the company you were working for?

Another set of reasons typically have to do more with you and your fit or aptitude for the *role, space* or particular situation. Maybe you lost the job due to some interpersonal issues of one kind or another. Perhaps you were just not that good at what you were doing or did not keep up with what was happening either politically or technically?

After losing a job, you might be tempted to blame the invisible powers of the world that have crashed the economy or the company. If you look a bit deeper, on the other hand, you might see that you could have guessed that something was going wrong and taken steps to prepare yourself for such an eventuality.

You also might be tempted to blame a certain person who never liked you or did you wrong in some way. Again, I find that a deeper analysis might link aspects of your own behavior to your relationships with others. If this is your situation, could you have managed the relationship differently and avoided the bad place you ended up in?

The most difficult situation is when you realize that you have lost your job due to your own mistakes or shortcomings. In 1985 my company made cuts because of the falling price of oil which I knew about but did not really process. I think I was put on list because I was not a great engineer in the first place and had made some mistakes.

In order to think through what has happened and why, you may need to gain some distance from the event itself and lose whatever resentment and anger you have bottled up. Such emotions are legitimate but can get in the way of thinking clearly and can have a negative impact on how you tell your story. I recommend going away for few days to allow your mind to sort things out.

How bad is it?

In 1985 I was in my 20s and had a couple thousand dollars in the bank. I sold my Honda Civic to my sister and took out a student loan to go to business school. You, on the other hand, probably have many more responsibilities, significant monthly expenses and mortgage payments or other debts to pay.

The first thing I suggest you do if you have just lost your job is to divide your savings by your total monthly expenses. This calculation will give you a number which indicates how many months leeway you have before you need to secure a new source of income.

If the number is somewhere between zero and six, then my advice is to find temporary work as soon as possible. The danger is that the financial stress you are under may cloud your judgment about what to do next. This could lead to you taking the first thing that comes along even if it is not the right position, the pay is not what you really want or if it is far from home.

Another aspect of financial stress is that it is difficult to hide and may put off potential employers. Your desperation might contaminate the interview process and make people uncomfortable. You may also try to rush a process which needs its time and fail to do the proper research into the position, company or people involved.

If you find yourself in this situation then the priority is to buy yourself some time. Doing a consulting project or working part-time can give you the space to think deeper about what you want to do and approach the job search in a more orderly and structured way.

If, on the other hand, you have either saved enough money or arrived at a reasonable settlement with your former company, then you may have 12, 18 or even more months in which to think about what to do next. In that case then losing a job can be a tremendous gift even if it does not currently feel like that.

Silver linings?

When I was nine, my father spent about a year between jobs, and my mother tells me that we spent every afternoon together building furniture in his small shop. He used the time to think through what he wanted to do in the next phase of his professional life. An added benefit was the time we were able to spend together which I think has made me a better man.

If you have lost your job and are feeling stress and anxiety, my advice is to recognize those emotions and deal with them in one way or another. Pretending that everything is fine will typically end up affecting some other aspect of your life.

When to Quit ?

Over the years many people have asked me if they should quit their current job. I have developed a list of 10 of the reasons they give:

1) Your work is making you ill or your boss is abusive or behaving inappropriately.

If your health is suffering or you find yourself in an abusive or inappropriate situation with respect to your direct supervisor, you should quit or take an immediate leave of absence and get away from the toxic environment. You should also document what is going on and perhaps find a lawyer to advise you.

In many firms, the human resource department has a process to deal with such situations, but they may be more focused on protecting the company than helping you. I understand this situation has improved thanks to the "me too" movement which has shone a needed spotlight on unacceptable behavior in the workplace.

2) You don't like or can't get along with your boss.

Short of abuse, you may have a very difficult relationship with your boss. I believe that almost anyone can be managed if you choose to understand where they are coming from and what their leadership style is. There are bosses who micromanage and others who delegate too much and everything in between. To make it work, you will have to adapt, and the real question is how far you are willing to go.

A senior partner once told me that the dress shirts I was wearing were inappropriate as they had a breast pocket and marked me as an engineer rather than an executive. While my first instinct was to get angry, I realized that I did not care which shirts I wore so I asked him where he bought his shirts and have worn similar ones since.

Many organizations develop a formal or informal set of leadership behaviors, and you want to be sure that you are comfortable with whatever the normal style is. If you happen to work for someone who has a particularly unpleasant style that is different from the norm, then you may want to wait them out as they probably will not last forever or transfer to a different part of the company or institution.

3) You don't like the boss.

A different case is if you really cannot get along with the owner or the country manager or CEO and know that they have the full support of the board. If this is the case then you probably do not agree with the basic values of the organization itself and should probably look for a new opportunity.

Companies and organizations do, however, evolve and a number of large companies like Microsoft and Bacardi have recently undergone a change in CEO and a deep process of cultural renewal. At the senior level, it may be worth working through scenarios of what would have to happen for the company to become a place you want to spend your time.

4) You feel underpaid

This is the most common complaint, and it is sometimes, but not always, true. Many companies suffer from an effect called compression in which the firm offers higher salaries to new people than what they paid a few years ago. This can create situations where seniors do not earn much more than juniors causing frustration. In other cases specific people such as cybersecurity experts are paid more than people who have been with the company for years.

The best thing to do in this instance is test the job market and get, but not necessarily accept, another offer. If a competitor will pay you 20 or 30 percent more for a similar combination of *role*, *space* and *place*, then you might want to think about leaving. If you do not find such an offer, then maybe you are already being paid in line with the market.

I would, by the way, treat the references you get from friends or specialized websites like Glassdoor with caution. People often overstate the money they make.

If a colleague is getting more money for what you consider to be similar work, then try and dig deeper to see what is going on. This could be, for example, because the firm sees more potential in them. If you do uncover an issue of prejudice, then you can either take the company to court, quit or just live with the injustice.

5) You have a better offer.

Before accepting an offer, I urge you to consider the benefits that your current employer may give you including things like social relationships, the ability to get things done and perhaps some connection with the values and purpose of the firm. If the offer comes with a large increase in pay, try to understand if that comes with additional responsibility or expectations. As they say, there is no such thing as free lunch.

What I never recommend is using another offer to try to get a raise from your present employer. A move like that can break the sense of trust that is so important in organizational life, and it may never be repaired.

I do, on the other hand, think its ok to tell your boss about an offer you have rejected as a way of gently suggesting that someday you would like a raise. Such a conversation needs to be had with delicacy but can be an opportunity to re-enforce the feelings of trust and shared purpose.

Having made a decision to leave, then I would always suggest having a serious, face-to-face meeting with your boss and to stick to the plan. They may try to talk you out of leaving or offer you more money to stay. If this happens keep in mind that they are trying to fix their problem, that is, how to survive without you, rather than worrying about your desire for better pay or more opportunity.

6) You are bored.

Many people come to see me because they feel that they are doing the same thing day after day and are learning nothing. If this is your situation, then the first idea is to try to change some aspect of the *role* to make it more interesting. In some cases your supervisor will be sympathetic to a conversation like this, and in others you may want to talk to human resources.

People in their 20s appear to be seeking more responsibility sooner than many organizations are prepared to give them. Part of the disconnect might stem from managers who spent years paying their dues and feel that "their" people should do the same. If this is the case then I would suggest recalibrating your expectations if you do feel you are in the right *space* and *place*.

You may have to be patient.

7) You are in the wrong *space*.

Like in the metaphor of the river, you may find that you really have little interest or passion for the *space* you find yourself in. You may find yourself in a related situation which is that you no longer believe that the *space* has any future at all due to changes in the business landscape.

In my view there is very little to be done in this case. Accept the fact and develop a medium-term plan to get out of that *space* and into something more interesting.

Take your time.

8) You see no role models.

A role model is someone who is 10–20 years ahead of you in their career and you consider to have a terrific combination of *space*, *role* and *place*. If there is no-one in your current organization that you admire then you may want to think about moving on.

One of the reasons I left management consulting is that I really did not look up to anyone in the organizations I was in. The senior partners were smart and wealthy but worked incredibly hard, and I did not feel I would be happy if I got that far.

9) You can't see your future.

In my view the best way to determine what your future in a specific company is to ask your supervisor, human resources or your mentor if you have one. The only problem with starting such conversations is that you may not like what you hear.

At one time I felt I was stuck in my consulting career. I was a senior principal and felt that I was not getting promoted to partner fast enough. At the time I had two bosses, a German and an Englishman, so I took advantage of meetings I had with each one to ask where they saw my career going.

The German told me to be patient. His view was that I was technically competent but had much to learn about client relationships. The Englishman told me that I would be better off considering a transfer to another part of the company. While I now realize that the German was right, I took the feedback as proof that my future was limited and left the company soon after.

10) You see or are expected to behave in unethical conduct.

On the issue of compliance, I learned from the CEO of a large automotive supplier that there is no gray zone in these cases. Things are either ok or not ok, and I would urge you to be clear on what that means for you. No one can pay you enough money to compromise your sense of right and wrong, and if you find yourself in such a situation then get out immediately.

There are some sectors, companies, and countries in which it is routine to make payoffs, kickbacks or facilitation payments. If you feel uncomfortable with such practices, then you may not have done enough homework before getting involved.

There are people who have the courage and conviction to become a change agent in their chosen field of endeavor. Taking on the role of reformer or whistleblower, however, requires a special mindset, and it might be easier just to do something else.

Search, Selection and Outplacement

For many people, the first thing that comes to mind when they begin thinking about changing jobs is to reach out to people in search or selection companies in the mistaken belief that they will get them another job.

Three things are important to understand about these firms. The first is that both types of firms find people for jobs not jobs for people.

The second idea is that both search and selection firms typically do well when putting people into a different company or *place* but tend to focus on people who already know how to play a specific *role* in a specific *space*. It is hard, although not impossible, to get them to think outside of that box.

Finally, it is also important to understand the difference between search and selection since the two businesses use different methodologies and tools.

Executive search is about understanding the challenges the newly hired executive will face and then *searching* for the right person. Search firms normally charge one-third of total annual compensation and work on a retained basis which means that their clients pay their fees regardless of whether the process is successful.

Selection agencies use advertising and internet job boards to identify potential candidates and then select those for their clients to meet. They charge a flat fee or a much lower percentage and are focused on saving the client time.

Most search consultants use the salary of a position as the way to distinguish between the two approaches. They may say, for example, that people earning $150,000 or more should be found by headhunters and that positions below that should be filled by using selection agencies. I disagree with this logic and instead use three tests to determine if a position should be filled using search or selection.

The first test is the total number of qualified people for the particular position. If there are only 5–10 people in the world who meet the criteria, then I would recommend using a search firm to find them and get them to consider the opportunity. If the number is, on the other hand, greater than 50 or more, then selection agencies are better positioned to reach out to them and process their applications.

The second test is to use a search firm if the person will have a major measurable impact on the business. If, on the other hand, the position is low risk or well supervised, then a selection firm will probably be adequate because a mistake can be remedied.

The third test is if anyone other than the hiring manager and human resources is really paying attention. Such a list includes shareholders, unions, government officials and the press. In such cases having the stamp of approval of one of the leading search firms could be helpful from a political or public relations point of view.

The search process

Most of the top headhunters follow a fairly standard process, and it is helpful to understand it.

The first step they take is to understand what the client needs. This is done in a series of meetings and ends up in a document which describes the position, the type of experience and skills that the company expects the candidate to have and any personal characteristics such as style or values that are important.

Personal details such as age, gender, ethnic group, and so on, are illegal in the United States and in many other countries, and such preferences are normally not documented if they exist at all.

The second step is to do the research and come up with a list of candidates. In most firms this step is performed by research associates. They find candidates by screening the web and their own database or phoning people up and asking for them to recommend others. They then proceed to screen candidates using preestablished criteria and make sure they are "open to talk" before passing them along to the partner doing the search.

The third step is where the partner does their evaluation of the candidates either through face-to-face meetings or virtually to see if they are right for the job. They then write a 1–2-page summary of the candidates' career and explore their "fit" to the position. A collection of such evaluations are presented to the client, and a decision is made on who they would like to meet.

The fourth step is where the client meets with a few people (often three) and decides which of the candidates, if any, they would like to hire.

The final step is negotiation and referencing during which the headhunter gets involved in helping to craft a compensation package acceptable to all sides and simultaneously conducts detailed reference checks to assure that everything they told the client about the candidate is true, and any surprising information is found out before the contract is signed.

The hard truth is that if you are looking for a job, you do not fit in this process until you are contacted by the research associate.

People complain about how difficult it is to talk with or meet headhunters and how some even do not bother to return emails or phone calls. While there is little excuse for being rude, the fact is that the probability that someone looking for work happens to match a project a headhunter is working on at a specific moment is very low.

When I was in this business, I would schedule such people on slow days and would do my best to be polite but also shatter any illusions they may have had about my ability to help. The most probable outcome of such a meeting is that the headhunter will listen to your story, tell you that they will be in touch if something opens up and pass your CV along to their research associate for coding into the database.

If you send your CV to the office (or any office in the firm), the result will be very close to the same. One of the newer research associates or administrative assistants will code your details into the database and put your CV into the system. There it will remain until the firm is asked to look for someone just like you, and your name is added to the list.

The reason that headhunters are very seldom able to help people who want to fundamentally change paths and do something new is that their clients are paying money to get a specific result. If a headhunter would say, "I know a great guy who does not have any experience in the field but ..." his client would probably be disappointed.

This only makes sense when there is a compelling logic. By that I mean that a candidate has specific skills or experience which make sense in a specific *role* or *place*. I once, for example, took a motor oil executive into the tire business since both sectors have similar dynamics on the ground, the products are not that different and the oil companies are thought to be better managed than the tire companies.

Only with this kind of logic is it really possible for a headhunter to present you for a *space* or *role* which is new to you.

Since not all of the people in this business have this much imagination, my advice is for you to think through that compelling logic and put it in a cover letter explaining why you think your story makes sense for a specific *space*, *role* and *place*.

Selection companies

The main issue to bear in mind when dealing with selection agencies is that the goal of the person you are interacting with is to reduce the number of people they put in front of their clients. Their challenge is that there are potentially hundreds of qualified candidates, and thus they need to reduce the pool in some rational way.

These firms use people or software to go through CVs they have received as well as job boards and LinkedIn to find qualified candidates and then to screen them out. It is therefore a good idea to keep your digital identity up to date and accurate. In this context it is important to avoid any obvious inconsistencies, mistakes or grammatical errors as they will put you in the reject pile.

The process at selection companies is typically run by more junior people with a less in-depth job and person specifications and research. Because of that, keep your cover letter and resume or CV as clear and informative as it can be and apply to as many companies as you can.

Outplacement agencies

I was sent to an outplacement agency after being laid off from my job as an engineer. I was provided with professional help in writing my CV, did mock interviews and was taught the ideas which later evolved to what I call intelligent networking and will be explained in detail in Chapter 10.

Such firms can give you a sounding board for thinking through what you want to do and practical advice such as which clothes to wear for an interview.

Lately this side of the business has expanded into a whole set of coaching-related disciplines including professional "life coaches" and even agents who take a similar view to business leaders as they do to athletes and film stars.

The most important thing to think through when dealing with any of these professionals is to remember that they are normally paid for by you and thus need to be responsive to your needs and offer a reasonable return for the money you pay them.

Landing the Job

Once you have a clear idea of what you want to do and are taking the steps to go out and do it, there are three things associated with the process which I will comment on. These are preparing your resume or CV, interviewing and negotiating the salary for your new position.

CV and cover letter

Writing your CV is more than simply cutting and pasting excerpts from your LinkedIn profile, and I have very strong ideas on the subject (see Box 8).

BOX 8: WRITING A CV OR RESUME

The resume needs to be relatively short and ideally one-page long. An exception is academic positions which are much longer.

A resume normally starts with your experience and includes the major jobs you have had indicating the title, the company you worked for and the time period you were there expressed in years. People love to see numbers in the small blurbs that go under each of your major positions, and these should be laid out in reverse chronological order.

People often mistakenly give the most space to the most recent position or the one for which they worked the most time. The vertical space which each job or phase takes up should vary based on the relevance that each position has for the job you are applying for.

The text under each position should be upbeat and use positive verbs to describe your accomplishments such as built, created or sold. It does, however, also need to be factual and properly reflect your role in achieving specific targets. Imagine that a recruiter would call your old boss and ask if what the resume says is true. If he or she would say yes, then your language is fine.

The idea is not to explain everything you did but to allow someone to use your CV to decide if they want to call you and then to guide them in conducting an interview with you. You only need to provide enough detail for them to understand what you were doing so they can ask their questions.

Academic qualifications and other skills such as languages should be listed in a separate section at the bottom of the page. My own view is that your personal goals and objectives should be described in a cover letter as you will probably explain your goals differently to different potential employers.

One thing to avoid at all costs is to put things that are not true in your CV. Not only do people exaggerate their accomplishments or their personal role in events but will even give themselves degrees they do not have or claim to be fluent in languages that they barely understand. These days such things are easy to check.

In some cases, it might be interesting to provide a list of projects or clients. I suggest adding such details as an appendix on separate pages so as not to interrupt the flow of the CV itself. For creative types, the project appendix could be done in a more creative style.

The last point on CVs is that the more experienced people are it seems that their CVs get simpler. Experienced managers often have a section titled "Early Career" which allows them to collapse 20 years of experience in to two or three lines.

For me, the resume is like a flyer for a Hunan-style restaurant which offers an all-you-can-eat buffet. It might give a small map and the phone number. The purpose of the flyer is to get you to walk over to the restaurant and look at the menu.

The purpose of the resume is to get a potential employer or the consultant working for them, to pick up the phone and invite you for an interview. It should be short and clear.

Cover letters should also be no longer than a page and cover the following topics:

● Why you are writing, that is, as a follow-up to call or in response to an add placed on such and such a date.

- What makes you qualified for the position?
- Why are you interested or even passionate about the opportunity and company?
- How they can reach you?

Another point is that if you are looking at different types of opportunities then you should write a different CV and cover letter for each. Remember, however, that although two CVs might have a different focus, they cannot contradict each other! The facts are the facts, and one cannot allow documents with different facts circulating in cyberspace.

Interviewing

If you make it through the filtering process, you may find yourself invited for an interview on the phone, over Zoom or face to face. Whatever the medium, there are a few key ideas which I believe are important to bear in mind.

The first idea is to be clear as to what type of interview you are in. In the first phases you may be contacted by a research associate or HR analyst whose job is to get further information from you and potentially screen you out of or into a process.

With these people my advice is to simply tell them the truth and see what happens. Their job is to make sure their boss only sees people who match a specific set of criteria. Try and help them.

The exception to this rule is if there is a compelling story which makes you qualified despite the lack of some specific experience or qualification. If you have such a story, tell it to the person on the phone and leave it up to them to pass it along or not. What would be even better is to get them to agree to allow you to send them an email explaining your ideas. This way, it is possible that the partner or the hiring manager will read your note.

A second type of interview is when your candidacy is being evaluated on by someone else on behalf of the person you will work for. These kinds of interviewers are usually experienced and will conduct the interview in a professional way.

When I worked as a headhunter, I would typically try to understand a person's professional progression. For each position, I would ask why they took the job, what they accomplished and learned and why they left. Be ready for these questions.

You will also be asked where do you want to be in the future and why you are interested in the particular combination of *space, role* and *place* that you are discussing.

In these kinds of meetings it is important to tell the truth as experienced interviewers will notice that something does not add up. They may not know exactly which part of the story is not accurate but will sense a false note. This will be enough for them to screen you out.

The third type of interview is when you finally talk with the people you are going to be working with, and this can include both the boss and other members of the team or executives in the company. In these meetings being honest is also important as is consistency. The people you meet will discuss your candidacy, and you should tell them all the same story about who you are, what you have done and why you are excited about the opportunity.

This last point may seem obvious, but if you are not excited by an opportunity, it is unlikely you will get the job. Interviewing for jobs you do not want not only is a waste of time but can make it more difficult to reach out to the same people in the future.

The best way to demonstrate your interest is by doing extensive research about the company and the people you are likely to meet. Look up their profiles and read anything they may have written or watch any videos they may have online.

A fantastic place to learn about a publicly traded company is in the investor presentations they often give to the community of financial analysts who follow them. I suggest watching such events in their entirety and taking detailed notes. If you do not feel you have time for this level of research, then I suggest you are not that interested in the opportunity.

The last reason for telling the truth throughout an interview process is that even if you did manage to fool everyone involved and get a job for which you are unprepared or unqualified, then you will be stuck pretending every day, and this is not a recipe for happiness or success.

Negotiating a new salary

The last point I want to discuss is negotiating your new salary.

I know one consultant who had the idea that you should fight hard to get the package you want before you start in a specific job or company as you will later be "locked in" to a set of rules about maximum raises, and so on. I disagree with this approach.

Most positions have a salary or salary range attached to them. Most hiring managers try to be fair when making job offers and will normally offer whatever is acceptable to them and their organization.

My advice is therefore to simply not "ask" for any specific level but to turn it around and urge the perspective employer to make the offer. Normally, there are three possible results to this technique. One is that you are delighted with the offer and accept it.

The other is that you find the offer unacceptable because it does not cover your financial needs. If this is the case, then there is probably some basic misunderstanding of either what your needs are or what the job actually can pay. Years ago, I flew to Europe for a job interview only to find that the headhunter had got my age wrong and that the company could not offer me the position that I had come to discuss.

The third and frequent situation is that the offer is acceptable but disappointing compared to your expectations. In this case my advice is to accept the job but request an official salary review after six months. The reason that this strategy works is that commitment costs the potential employer nothing but, if things do go well, creates an obligation for them to act later on or at least "owe you one."

Tough negotiations at the start, however, may sour your relationship with your new employer or some other staff members at a delicate moment. If there is a third party involved, such as headhunter, I recommend that they do the back and forth to avoid any embarrassment and minimize the potential for misunderstandings.

The best approach is to accept the position before you know what the money will be. This option only works when you are going to take the job in any case. The idea is your trust will motivate your future employer to do the best for you within whatever limits they are under.

Key Ideas Chapter 8

- Getting fired or laid off is difficult for most people, and you may need to channel your frustration, anger or disappointment in some way.
- The process of looking for a new job can be extremely stressful but is also an enormous opportunity to take control over your professional life.
- If you need to make money in the short term, consider temporary or part-time work in order to keep bread on the table while finding the right position.

- It is important to reflect on the reasons why you want to make a change, and unless you are in a terrible situation, it is usually better to find a new job before quitting the old one.
- Headhunters and selection agencies can help but will mainly recommend you for positions you have already had.
- Pay attention to your digital profile, CV and cover letters to assure that they are accurate, consistent and well written.
- Prepare well for any interviews and know your own story.

CHAPTER 9

CHANGING PHASES

In the previous chapter, I wrote about changing jobs assuming that you would continue with the current phase of your professional life. This chapter is about doing something that is fundamentally different either because you choose to or have been pushed into it by changes to your personal circumstances, the pandemic or other major shifts.

Such changes typically involve changes to *space, role* or *place* or perhaps more than one of these dimensions. Changing all three at once is the biggest challenge of all. It is like a freestyle skier who jumps, spins and does a somersault all at the same time.

Many people have found that they change their profession a few times during their life. In my own story, I have been an engineer, management consultant and business school professor and within each larger phase have had different jobs or positions in different organizations.

I started my consulting phase, for example, as a generalist in the Madrid office of an American company. That firm then moved me to Boston where I specialized in innovation and automotive. I then came back to Spain with a different firm as an automotive specialist. The last step in this phase was to learn a new *role*, headhunting, but in the same *space*, that is, the global automotive business.

One of the key points that Gratton and Scott make in *The 100-Year Life* is that as we live longer it will be normal to have different professional phases.

If you are looking to make such a change, I have found five ways to do it. One is to make the change in your present organization. A second is to make it happen through what I call active networking. A third is to start by doing a project or a gig to gain credibility, and the fourth is to start your own business. A fifth path that will be discussed in Chapter 10 is to go back to school.

Changing Phases in Your Current Company

The difficulty of finding an opportunity in a new *space*, *role* and *place* at the same time cannot be overstated. Would you hire someone for a job if they have no experience in the *space*, *role* or *place*?

One place where you might be given such a chance is with your present employer. What you bring is a deep understanding of how your company works and what is even more important the trust and confidence of people at head office. In some cases such an assignment may be a deliberate attempt to stretch your abilities and prepare you for greater things in the future.

From management's viewpoint, it is often easier to teach a person they know and trust a new skill, than to try and find the person with that skill who happens to fit in with the culture of the firm. In some fast-growing markets and product categories, there simply are no experts in the business itself, and anyone who does it will have to learn on the job!

As companies around the world come to grips with the new normal, they are rethinking the businesses they are in and how to organize them. Some firms will exit certain *spaces* and get into new ones. This is actually a very good time to make sure that you are one of the people that the company will choose to keep regardless of what happens to your unit or division.

The trick is to find the right way to let the organization know that you are not fully happy with your current role and signal what you would like to do. Expressing dissatisfaction alone can be professionally risky, and I do not recommend you do it. Having your own view of the future and how you think you can add more value to the organization as a whole, on the other hand, can be seen as positive.

If you have already decided to pursue a new course in any case, then you don't have much to lose to try by trying your present employer first. I would even say that if the company has treated you reasonably well, then you at least owe the people involved a chance to keep you. You can do that by carefully sharing what you want to get involved with specific people and then allowing them to explore whether it could be possible.

I have seen and experienced six basic ways to do this, and I will go through each one.

Talk to your current boss

Probably the most effective way to get a different job is to tell your boss what you are interested in and ask for their help. If they are genuinely interested in you and understand that developing people is part of their job, then this strategy is the best.

There are only two real problems if you have a boss like this: One is that they might try to talk you out of what you want to do because they really feel it would be a mistake on your part. The other is that they will probably promise to do what they can but also ask you to be patient because at least for the next 3–6 months, they will need you to stay where you are. In either case, the key is to be ready for such a response and either accept their advice or stick to your idea and be gently insistent!

If your boss is more concerned with themselves or the short-term needs of their part of the business, they could react badly to your request and even see it as an act of disloyalty. If this is the reaction, then it tells you something about that person and perhaps the overall culture of the firm.

Talk to your "new" boss

Another option is to go visit the person responsible for the part of the business you want to join and ask for a job. The tricky part of this plan is to have the right kind of access to that person and ensure that they have some sort of understanding of who you are and what you are capable of.

Most managers are looking for talented people so the response to this kind of approach will generally be positive but noncommittal. Positive because in fact it might be a good idea but noncommittal because until they know what the reaction of your current manager, human resources, and others in the organization is that they will not want to commit. They might also want to get some internal references on you.

Talk to your mentor (if you have one)

Assuming you have access to a someone who is senior to you but is not your direct supervisor, a terrific way to seek out new opportunities is to go to that person and share your thoughts and see what they have to say. They should be able to see beyond your current role and think about what's best for the organization and your own development.

Ideally they will have enough authority, experience and political power to set things in motion which will result in getting you a new appointment.

The only warnings are to be sure about trusting in that person and also to be clear about what you want to do. On this last point, you might also involve them in your thinking process.

Work with the human resources people

Many companies have an excellent human resources function who keep a detailed inventory of the talent in the organization and take an active role in proposing people for international assignments and rotation across the company.

If you work in such an organization then my advice is to be clear about your hopes and aspirations but recognize that while human resources will want to help, their first loyalty is to the firm and not to you.

In that context, if in fact you "are needed" where you are, then they will most likely "take note" of your needs and keep their eyes open for a way to fulfill them, while at the same time, avoiding conflict with your current supervisor.

If you work for a firm in which the human resources organization is not very strong, then I would be very careful on how much to say to them during the early stages of such a process. Later on they will become involved in issues such as salary, bonus and relocation expenses.

One important point about financial conditions has to do with who is asking who for the move. If the company requests that you move, then it makes sense for you to ask for compensation in one form or another. If, on the other hand, the perception is that you are asking for the move, the general trend will be to "accommodate" your interests, but perhaps it will be difficult to get a raise or relocation allowance.

Talk to the boss

Another technique is to go all the way to the top and ask the boss, CEO or the president. Of course, there are obvious dangers to this approach but if, in fact, the organization is largely driven by one person who will make the decision anyway, then a direct approach might make sense.

Naturally, the first question they will ask you is if you have spoken to your boss about this idea, and you will need a really good reason if you have not.

If circumstances permit, the best ways to make this happen is to arrange to "bump into" the CEO or meet on something completely unrelated and have the new opportunity come up in conversation. Since it is seemingly spontaneous, then it makes sense not to have had a chance to speak with your boss yet. The logical next step would be then for you to go do that but "at the request" of the CEO.

Send a message

If none of the above paths are found to be appealing in a specific situation, then the only option open is to send a message through one or several third parties. By sending a message I refer to finding an excuse to meet with or talk to some other people and let them know how you feel to some extent.

One way to do this is to speak with a friend at your level who works in the area you would like to go to. Tell them how much you envy them. If the relationship permits, then simply crying on their shoulder may be enough to trigger a series of conversations which eventually might lead to a new role for you.

In this way one could, potentially, send several parallel messages to senior management which would put your name "in play" and then allow you to consider a new opportunity when finally asked. In essence what one does is to invite different people to assume some type of mentorship role even if your relationship with them had not been so before.

BOX 9: MISSION CRITICAL LEADERSHIP

Within the phases discussed above there may be a number of steps or specific jobs or positions. These jobs might happen in one or several companies and sometimes a person's job might change while keeping the same title.

To explore this idea further, I use a framework developed by the late Paddy Miller who was my friend, role model and mentor. Miller developed the framework based on executives from Hewlett Packard and makes the case that many assignments last 1,000 days or even less. His insight was that if we know from the start that our time in a job is limited, then our goals, objectives and leadership style will be different than if we assume it is open ended.

The model is particularly well suited for managers and is less applicable to scientists, doctors and academicians.

Miller divided these 1,000 days into what he called three windows.

Miller called the first 200 days of a new job the window of opportunity. In this period you will be full of energy and set out to learn what you need to know about the new position, the team and the overall environment. At some point it will be necessary to come up with plan and communicate it to your boss and the team. You should also be able to find some quick wins which helps build credibility and momentum.

Miller called the next 300 days the window of efficiency. At this time one of the key issues is typically the performance of the team and your relationships with other people in the organization, key customers and so on. Typically this is where you may have to begin to manage the initial expectations and also make sure your results are becoming sustainable.

Miller called the last 500 days of a specific position the window of achievement. In his view the key things to think about are developing a clear successor, making sure that the powers that be understand you to have been successful in the position, and to work out what to do next.

To see if the model fits your own professional life, you can divide the number of years you have been working by the number of different positions or jobs you have held and multiply by 365. You should get a number which is typically between 500 and 1,500 depending on how old you are and how often you have changed jobs.

In terms of changing jobs, if you have been in the same role for more than 3–4 years, then you may want to think about what is holding you back? Can someone else take over from you? Are you considered to have been successful? Do you know what you want you to do next?

Networking and Social Media

Although headhunters and selection consultants have difficulty recommending people with little or no experience in a given field, there are others who are often delighted to make such connections. These are people like independent board members, former professors, friends and acquaintances. They are often asked if they "know someone" by an executive looking to fill a particularly sensitive or urgent position.

The key difference between them and the professionals discussed above is that they are not getting paid for the service and therefore are free to recommend anyone they like. The issue is how to get to such people. Meeting them, either physically or virtually, and getting them to recommend you to others is what I call intelligent networking.

It's about the network not you

Unintelligent networking is to write or call a contact who works at a company you are interested in and ask if there is a job for you there. You probably have received a call like that and answered something like "I don't think we are hiring right now but why not send me your C.V. and I'll pass it along." All CV's received like this go to human resources and often end up filed away and forgotten. The process is a waste of time and often leads to embarrassment and disappointment.

My daughters once had a video game about a small space adventurer who was a talking fox. He had been sent to save Dinosaur Planet from a bunch of bad dinosaurs. To advance in the game one had to move around the bad dinosaurs' fortress, but this was difficult because it was heavily guarded by lasers and heavily armed bad dinosaurs.

At one point in the game, however, you can acquire a dinosaur disguise which temporarily allows the fox to have free run of the fortress and thus be able to complete a phase in the mission to save the planet.

The point is that networking has very little to do with using your network of contacts, friends and acquaintances and everything to do with penetrating a new network just like the fox in the dinosaur fortress.

In every *space* and *place* in the world there is already a tightly woven network of professionals who mostly know one another.

Think about advertising executives in Berlin, magazine publishers in New York City or automotive executives in Detroit. The number of people who own and manage these firms is actually pretty low. If you could meet with some proportion of such people in a given network, then it becomes likely that they would know about most significant opportunities in that *space* and *place*.

I find the best way to reach these people is not to ask for a job but to ask for advice. They will ask you how they can help and eventually will ask you to tell them your own story. As discussed in Chapter 3, your story needs to be interesting, compelling and above all sincere.

Such meetings often look and feel like job interviews for which there is no specific job. If you can think of reasonable questions to ask and present yourself as bright, hardworking and a quick learner, they might even try to help you break into their circle.

If you can get each person to give you two additional people to meet with, then, over time, you will soon meet with dozens of people from the network. The best outcome is when you eventually are sent to see a very highly placed person in the company you most admire and they say "Well why not work here?"

The best thing about this technique is that every meeting will make you a bit smarter about the new *space* and thus improve your ability to speak its language, know who's who, and so on. I have counseled many people to use this technique over the years, and there are only a couple of key rules to making it work.

The first is to be as specific as possible in knowing which *space* you are most interested in. You need to exhibit a passion for it which cannot be faked.

Doing extensive research on the *space* and everyone you meet with is the second rule. With the power of the internet there is no excuse to not being fully briefed on any company and almost on any person.

The final rule is to be yourself and be pretty open with who you are and what you think you can bring to the *space*. In fact this could be part of your questions!

The main reason the method works is that when faced with people who are truly passionate about something our natural impulse is to try and help them. What's even more important is that by recommending such people to others we are actually doing a favor for both because most managers are looking for good people all the time.

The downside to this technique is that it does take a lot of time and energy. Three to six months is, for example, a reasonable time frame to begin to make traction in a new *space* and *place*.

What will make this process a little bit easier is most managers and executives have spent a lot more time on Zoom, Skype and Teams in the last year or two than ever before. This has made them more receptive to having conversations with people virtually rather than face to face.

In the past, I would have counseled someone to tell a potential contact that they are planning to be in town in the next month or so and would like to meet for a cup of coffee or tea. These days, you can ask for a 10–15 minutes on Zoom.

Although this may sound obvious, digital meetings need to be prepared as well or better than physical ones. Be on time, dress appropriately and make sure your video and audio set up is crisp and professional.

Social media

Social media is increasingly used as an initial connection point in this kind of process, and there are entire books written about how to use platforms like LinkedIn to land a job.

As discussed in Chapter 9, having a well-crafted digital profile is a requirement these days but will not, by itself, attract a recruiter. On the LinkedIn platform you can also follow specific companies and interest groups and your activity in these spaces is often tracked by recruiters. If you are serious about a specific company, then following them makes sense as would looking at their Twitter and Instagram feeds.

What can be done even more to open up new doors is being active in the blogosphere by building a twitter following or posting blogs on a topic of interest. Such activity can be very time-consuming but can add to your credibility in a *space* which is a bit outside your current job description.

If you do choose to venture into this kind of activity, then I highly recommend getting some training or reading about the best ways to behave online. You want to make sure that you respect the norms and standards on platforms such as Twitter and LinkedIn just like you would try to be polite in face-to-face environments.

Such platforms are the digital equivalent of participating in events and congresses and giving speeches on your topics of interest. If possible, such activity is also a terrific way of demonstrating your interest in a *space* and *place* and eventually getting known by people in the network.

Reaching out directly to very senior people on social media is, in my view, the equivalent of walking up to such people in a congress or live event. Normally you would only do so if you have a prior appointment, are recommended by someone else or have something very specific to say. Just like in the physical world, my advice is to contact the executive assistants of such people and ask them for a meeting or perhaps the name of someone else in the organization who you should talk to first.

Perhaps the last comment on social media which may seem obvious is to be careful with what you put out there. At one level, you need to be sure that any different versions of your CV are consistent with each other. As mentioned earlier, they can have different emphasis but need to have the same facts.

The other issue is to make sure there is nothing compromising about you on the web. You may feel that your personal life should have nothing to do with your professional image, and while I agree with that idea in principle, social media is not private and some potential employers look at such things.

It is, by the way, unlikely that the potential employer will ask you about any pictures or statements that they found objectionable for whatever reason. They are more likely to reject your candidacy for some other reason in order to avoid having to ask about sensitive matters.

Gigs and Projects

Beyond the idea of using short-term projects as a bridge or a stop gap measure discussed in Chapter 9, many people have adopted the model as their permanent form of working.

In the 1930s and early 1940s directors and actors were on permanent contracts with the Hollywood's leading movies studios such as Warner Brothers. Humphrey Bogart, for example, made dozens of films for Warner Brothers before the contract system was phased out in the late 1940s and replaced by the current practice of hiring actors on a freelance basis.

Besides actors, virtually the entire production and editing crew of a modern motion picture is made up of temporary people and outsourced firms which in turn hire the artistic and technical people required.

There has been a similar pool of talent in the automotive business for many years. It takes several hundred engineers to design a new car not to mention the engineers who develop the systems and components that make up a modern automobile.

Most of the major car companies deliberately employ significantly less engineers than they need in order to assure a steady workflow for the people on staff. When the company is busy on a number of new models at the same time, they tap into the network of engineers and designers who move around the industry from project to project.

There is also a branch of the executive search business, called interim management, which deals with short-term assignments for senior executives. Such positions often have to do with specific tasks like opening or closing a manufacturing plant or implementing a specific project or program.

Interim executives typically get paid 20–30 percent more than they would make in a full-time role, but the company also saves money in the long run as it only needs their specialized experience for a relatively short time.

Daniel Pink[1] has written about how this idea is now being extended to even broader parts of the economy. This phenomenon, that Pink wrote about almost 20 years ago, is typically referred to as *the gig economy*. It is said to represent as much as 10 percent of the workforce in the United States.

As discussed by Louis Hyman,[2] an economic history professor at Cornell, temporary working arrangements have been increasing since the 1960s and represent a fundamental shift in the way the economy works. He places management consultants and advisers at the top of the pecking order in the gig economy and day laborers at the bottom.

In the last few years, it has been particularly associated with relatively new *spaces* such as games design, software developers, cybersecurity and data

1   D. Pink, *Free Agent Nation: The Future of Working for Yourself* (Chicago: Business Plus, 2001).
2   L. Hyman, *Temp: The Real Story of What Happened to Your Benefits, & Job Security* (2019).

mining. It has also been extended to new and fast-growing *roles* in the peer-to-peer service business such as driving for Uber or Lyft or managing Airbnb apartments.

Working gigs can be rewarding but does have a downside that needs to be well understood.

The light and the dark

The proponents of the gig economy discuss the freedom such work can give you, the idea that you have no boss and that you can do many of these jobs in parallel with other, more creative activities.

When speaking with Uber and Lyft drivers, you will find that many of them are aspiring actors, musicians or digital types who drive in their spare time to either "keep busy" or perhaps be able to pay the rent. A friend who is a professional jazz musician told me that back in his time, every decent musician in New York spent some time as a cabdriver. He said it was like a rite of passage.

For many people who lost their jobs as a result of the pandemic and economic crisis in 2020, the gig economy was the only immediate path to finding any paid work which could help pay the rent and keep food on the table.

While the basic nature of these *roles* are not new, what is different is the ease with which digital technologies allow people to find them and also the way they are managed.

The first problem with working in the gig economy is that there is no safety net when things go badly for the company or the economy as a whole.

In the United States, full employment fell by 22 million during March and April 2020, and this number does not include temporary workers who lost about half of their jobs or saw their income drop sharply as a result of the pandemic.[3] Fortunately, the economy came back in 2021, but this does not change the hardship that many families experienced during the worst part of the crisis.

The second problem with the gig economy is that companies typically provide little-to-no benefits to gig workers since they are not technically employees of the firm. In some cases independent contractors work alongside salaried employees and do essentially the same work for less money, less security and no health care. In March 2019, *The New York Times* reported that Google had more temps and contractors than full-time employees (54 percent), and a number of

---

3   The Fair Work Project, *The Gig Economy and Covid-19: Looking Ahead* (2020).

studies have shown that the trend is common at Apple, Facebook, Amazon and their smaller competitors.

Mary Gray and Siddharth Suri[4] coined the term "the ghost economy" to describe the tens of thousands of people who do much of the work upon which many successful digital business models are based. Their focus is the people who assist the algorithms in many of the world's most successful apps.

The delivery companies have also been called out for offering very low pay, no benefits and a heartless and mechanical attitude to the people who actually deliver the goods.

Part of the issue is that the day-to-day management of these activities is done by algorithms that give people their assignments, rate their performance and pay them as a function of supply and demand. What is missing is the Danny DeVito character from *Taxi*, an old television series, who acted like a tough guy but really did care about the drivers as people.

In academia, the equivalent are adjunct professors who do not receive the same (if any) health care benefits, can never get tenure and are treated as second-class citizens by their colleagues who are "on the faculty."

Pink saw how companies could avoid paying benefits and investing in training by allowing armies of freelancers to do much of the work that used to be done by their own staff. The gig economy may bring you freedom but at the cost of stability.

Just for now

Many people in their 20s are working in the gig economy since doing a series of short-term gigs can provide enough money to move out of the family home or maybe save up and go traveling.

In the context of a 100-year life with several different professional phases, I think it makes sense for people in their 20s to pause and experience a number of things before setting out on a specific course.

Young men and women have been working at language schools, ski slopes, tourist hotels, scuba diving centers and other such places for years and is certainly not new. I always thought that it would be a lot of fun to be a ski instructor, boat captain or dive instructor for a few years. The problem is that I have met people in their 30s and 40s who feel they have been doing such jobs for

---

4 M. Gray and S. Suri, *Ghost Work: How to Stop Silicon Valley from Building a New Global Underclass* (Boston: Mariner Books, 2019).

much too long and have difficulties making ends meet or offering their families a certain degree of stability.

If this last kind of work is your passion, then I think there are two reasonable choices as you get older. One is to do it on a recreational basis while you do something else to make a living. The other is to go all in and open a diving center or ski school or buy a boat and put it out for charter. Starting your own business is the subject of the next section.

Entrepreneurship

In some cases, the best way to solve the equation of *space* and *place* is to assume the role of *entrepreneur* and start your own business. One way to articulate this is to take the gig economy one step further and rather than work without a boss, become the boss.

One of my cousins, for example, is a video artist who has worked with the same lighting and sound technicians in Los Angeles for years. Just before the pandemic he was trying to decide if he should rent his own studio space and lease expensive equipment. To do so he had to secure some seed money and open a production company.

A question he was struggling with is what to do about the team? One idea would be to leave things as they are but maybe they would not be available for an important contract. Another would be to offer them some form of partnership in the new business and a third would be to put them on salary. His issue with the third option is the responsibility he would have to assume and what becoming the boss might do to his relationships with the different people.

I distinguish between three types of entrepreneurs. The first opens what I call a lifestyle business. The basic idea is to build a business which can give you the combination of money, fulfillment and lifestyle you want to have.

A friend, for example, runs five coffee shops with about 50 employees and total revenue of about $3.5 million. A few years ago he asked me to help him grow the business but then decided not to when he realized that going to the next step would take him farther away from the people in the shops and his family.

Franchising is a well-established pathway to such a business and might be right for you. In exchange of paying the franchise fee and making the required investment, you receive training and support from the brand. If the location is well chosen and the concept successful, this can be a relatively safe and satisfying way of being your own boss and also providing jobs for others.

A second type of entrepreneur is interested in building something big. Typically this means setting up a business which requires significant capital and can sometimes only be done with other people's money. These kinds of businesses are often launched by executives from a particular *space* who have a vision of how things could be and the experience and contacts required to pull it off.

I would put most of the people stating web-based start-ups in a third category as their logic is a little different than a "normal" business.

In the start-up world, the idea is to be able to create something with very little capital and some good ideas. According to my colleague Chris Zott, the emergence of so many start-ups over the last few years is mainly due to the way digitalization has lowered the minimum scale required to get into many *spaces*. While it used to cost millions to develop a new product or service and build out the required infrastructure, one can now get in the game for under $50,000 or even less.

The initial money is typically raised from people the founders know and affectionately call friends, family and fools. Crowdfunding platforms such as Kickstarter can also raise initial capital for these types of adventures.

In this kind of start-up, the initial investment is needed only to flesh out the idea. After that, more money is needed to see if it will work and then even more to build the initial product and win the first customers. Each round of financing is approached with the idea of growing the business and its capabilities enough to get to the next step in the process.

If you are thinking of taking such a step be sure to choose your investors with care. While you might find a business angel who will invest their money and give you advice and counsel, take care to avoid business devils who will deliberately underinvest in order to gradually take control over your project every time you ask them for more money.

Timing is everything

After an economic crisis many of the inputs on the cost side of a business such as rent, staff and other up-front costs may have gone down. On the other hand, demand has also dropped in many *spaces* so it is all about getting the timing right.

If you have been fired or laid off, you might have the time you need to finally to talk with potential suppliers, partners and customers and write the business plan you have been thinking about.

Going back to the idea of intelligent networking, one of the best ways to get to know the people in a given *space* and *place* is to talk to them about your idea for a new business. What is really interesting is that the people you would need to talk to are mostly the same ones who you would want to talk to anyway if you were looking for a job.

The difference is that by looking at starting something new, your side of the story will be more interesting. What you might find in the course of your research is that someone tells you that your idea is a good one and they would like you to do it from within their organization!

The importance of passion

For all three of these kinds of businesses there are a number of relevant books, courses and online forums to go to learn more about them. In my experience what is sometimes missing from all of this is the question of passion.

To start with, the level of passion and energy of the management team is one of the key things that venture capitalist look for in a start-up. More importantly, new businesses will end up in one of the three outcomes.

Your business may succeed and provide you and your family with a steady income. It might even take off, be the next big thing and bring you financial wealth.

It is more likely, however, that the business will fail and the investment capital will be lost. If your personal investment was low, then you may be able to see the time and energy spent as an important learning experience. The good news about failure is you will get your life back, and there is something to be said for failing fast.

The real problem, however, is that the majority of new ventures neither succeed nor fail quickly. Such projects endure over time and always require more time, more money and more energy to get them to the next level or "across the chasm."[5] They are like black holes that suck in everything around the founder's life including their money, their relationship with each other and others and even their health.

The one thing that can make all three outcomes better is passion for the product, service or the *space* itself. In the first place, truly passionate people will have more probability of success as they will put more energy into the project, sell the idea better and inspire their colleagues to go the extra mile. True

---

5 Geoffrey A. Moore, *Crossing the Chasm: Marketing and Selling High-Tech Products to Mainstream Customers* (New York: Harper Business, 1991).

passion will also help if things do not go well as the learning will have more value if you really care about what you were trying to do.

Finally, for those businesses that do take a long time to come to fruition, then only deep passion, and maybe faith in a higher power, can give you the strength to carry on. If you are actually doing what you most love anyway, then maybe a lower level of financial success is OK anyway!

Step by Step

The last idea about changing phases is that it might make sense for you to first change one aspect of your current professional life and then move on to the next in a series of steps. The idea is to be like a billiards or pool player who normally takes the next shot only after thinking about the one after that.

Perhaps a first step is to change *roles* in the same *space* and *place* thus being able to capitalize on contacts and tacit knowledge about the sector. This is particularly relevant if you like the company and have the trust of senior management.

Another option is to keep *role* and *space* the same but do the same thing in a different *place*. Such an opportunity might come through for current employer through their established rotation program or by reaching out to headhunters.

The third choice is to stay in the same *place* and do the *role* you currently do in a different *space*. This will make the most sense if the *space* you are going to is dealing with similar issues than the one you come from. In this way you will be adding value because of your experience in the other *space* which has already gone through the transition.

A reasonable plan might be to make several moves over a 6- to 10-year period until eventually you are able to pursue your ideal combination of *space*, *role* and *place*.

This type of plan will appeal to you if you feel that you have too many financial or family constraints to take unnecessary risks. Another useful idea can be to go back to school to learn things you may need to know and perhaps acquire some accreditation to help build your credibility in a new *space*. This topic will be discussed at length in Chapter 10.

Key Ideas Chapter 9

• Your current employer is often the best opportunity for you to change the *space* you work in, the *role* you play and maybe the *place* you live and work.

- Networking can be a powerful way to break into a new space but needs to be done in a systematic and intelligent way.
- Working on a project on a gig basis can provide needed income and can also give you experience in a new role or space which will make you more credible later on.
- The gig economy does, however, have a downside that needs to be considered if it becomes a long-term option.
- In some cases starting your own business is the best way to get everything aligned.
- The process of researching a business plan will bring you into contact with interesting people in any case and can sometimes open interesting doors.
- In many cases the best way to change *space*, *role* and *place* is to do so one at a time in a step-by-step approach.

CHAPTER 10

LIFELONG LEARNING

Many years ago, the coach of Notre Dame's football team was quoted as saying "When the going gets tough, the tough get going." In the world of higher education, a different take on the quote would be that when the going gets tough, the tough go to graduate school!

Applications for MBAs, for example, normally increase in times of economic crisis, and 2020 and 2021 have been no exception. Losing a job is an opportunity to invest in your own education, and I made a similar choice in 1985 when I lost my job and went to business school.

The one constant in the future will be change, and you will need to acquire new knowledge and skills during your professional life. This will be particularly critical when you choose to move from one *role* to another, move to a new *space* or transition from one phase to the next.

Education can help you understand a new field, give you the chance to rub shoulders with people who are already in that business or at the very least provide objective proof that you have done something in a specific area and are therefore qualified for consideration.

Options include university degrees at the undergraduate and graduate levels, specialized programs offered in law, medicine and business, and so on, as well as all technical fields. There are also a host of shorter, face-to-face courses in everything from strategy and leadership to full stack coding and data analytics.

In managerial fields, many people choose to do an MBA or one of a number of nondegree, executive education programs. At both levels, there are a number of options available for you regardless of your age, money or time available. There are, however, legitimate questions about the value of timeless managerial concepts such as finance, marketing, strategy and leadership in a world which is changing so fast.

One argument is that by the time knowledge is captured, processed and made available in the university, it might already be out of date, particularly in technological fields which are changing very rapidly. A counter argument runs that a classical education is more important than ever because it will teach the critical reasoning needed in an ever-changing world.

Another discussion has to do with the merits of face-to-face education, the significantly cheaper e-learning platforms, and just reading up on whatever interests you. I, for example, offer a sustainability elective in the second year of the full-time, MBA program at IESE Business School and some of the same material in a ten-hour, online course on the Coursera platform and talk about the same ideas in a book, *Strategy & Sustainability*.

Face-to-Face Education

One way to get the education you need is to physically go to programs offered by universities, institutes and training companies. The advantage of face-to-face education is learning from other students in class no matter what their age and experience levels are. My conviction is that the job of a professor in today's world is not so much transmitting knowledge but giving people a framework in which they can interact with each other on a given topic.

After a brief discussion of undergraduate education, I will discuss master's programs and other types of adult education. In these two latter sections, I will discuss examples from my work at the business school not because business education is more important than other branches of human knowledge but only because it is what I know best, and the essential ideas can then be applied to courses in other fields such as sociology or science.

Undergraduate education

In the United States, people with a college education make more money, live longer and healthier lives and say that they are happier than people who do not. The cost of going to college has, however, skyrocketed over the last 20 years or so making it more difficult for people with less money to go. These two trends have led to increasing income inequality and social divisions across the country.

If you can afford it, the investment in time and money is still worthwhile even if wages have not kept pace with the increasing costs (see Box 10). If for whatever reason you did not go to college in your early 20s (like about

50 percent of Americans), I would seriously consider taking advantage of the many programs offered for older students by most schools.

BOX 10: THE VALUE OF A COLLEGE EDUCATION

Prior to the onset of the pandemic, in 2019, US house of Congress released a report[1] which outlined the benefits of a college education. According to the report, the cost of a going to college as increased by 81 percent since 1990 while median household income only increased by 12 percent.

Tuition, fees, room and board was $ 18,383 at public institutions and $ 47, 419 at private nonprofit schools in the 2018–19 academic year.[2]

Forty-eight percent of Americans between 25 and 34 have an advanced degree of one kind or another. According to the report, they will earn approximately $ 1 million more over their lives than people a high school degree. This is partly explained by increased demand for a host of positions for which an undergraduate or 2-year associate degree are requirements.

If the economic argument was not sufficient, there is also evidence that people with more education lead longer, healthier lives than people with less. Health does correlate with income but the gap in life expectancy has been increasing since the 1960s and was found to be on the order of 10 years or more deepening on which study and if you consider men, women and different ethnic groups.

What people are studying also gives a sense of the link between a college education and certain parts of the economy. In the academic year 2016–17, there were almost 2 million undergraduate degrees awarded in the United States. Business, health care, engineering, and biomedical sciences represented more than half of those degrees.

---

1 U.S. House of representatives, Committee on Education and Labor, Don't Stop Believin' in the Value of a College Degree (2019).
2 National Center for Education Statistics. Accessed June 27, 2021.

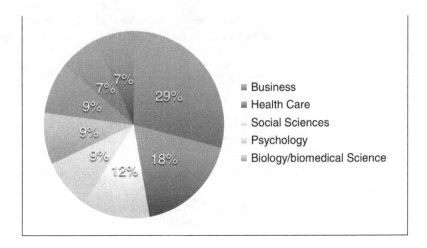

At first glance, the time, money and energy associated with such programs may seem daunting. You may also feel that the subject matter is not up to date or that the professors have little to teach you. While both these ideas might be true, there is a deeper issue at play that has to do with opportunity.

The reality is that most senior people in business and finance did go to college, and they favor others who do so. Many companies recruit their staff from the leading colleges and universities under the logic that if a student was accepted into such a school in the first place, they must be smart and/or hard working.

In a similar way, people who put themselves through school at a later stage in their life earn the respect of managers for having the grit and dedication needed to do get through such a course.

I strongly recommend studying a subject only for which you have a great deal of interest and passion as it will make it much easier to put in the hard work required. If you are not sure of what that is, then take some extra time to find out. In the context of living a long life, then another six-month delay will not be as important as actually getting on with it.

Masters programs

Both of my daughters have done their undergraduate and master's degrees in fields other than management. They studied what they were interested in as undergraduates, went to work for a few years and then went to a master's program that they thought would prepare them for what they really wanted to do.

The programs gave them the depth they needed to get into the field of their choice as well as a degree from a well-respected institution. The programs also allowed them to meet like-minded students from other backgrounds and think through how they wanted to make their own mark in the world.

The same logic applies to students who choose to do the master's in business administration or MBA. If you are interested in learning about different MBA programs, the website Poets and Quants is an outstanding place to go for general information and has detailed profiles of dozens of top schools.

The main reason that many of our students do an MBA is that it is something of a requirement in certain *spaces* and companies. Senior people in many consulting firms, investment banks and multinationals all have an MBA and often recruit from the leading schools.

A second reason is to meet interesting and potentially influential people. While classmates can, over the long term, become important in our personal and professional lives, the real value lies in being able to access the alumni network of the top schools.

The third good reason to do an MBA or any other advanced degree is if you find yourself having time on your hands and are not sure about what to do next. An industry slowdown, changes in one's personal situation or family life or some other reason may create a window of opportunity where one simply has a year or two to do something else, and such opportunities are relatively rare. For many people the global pandemic has provided that opportunity, although the classroom experience has, of course, suffered because of it.

In my own case, I had already decided to do an MBA eventually and took advantage of losing my job to do it sooner. I wanted to do an MBA is because I realized that I was never going to be a great engineer and wanted to do something in sales or management.

The MBA is a natural, well-established transition point where the global business community not only allows people to make a change but actually expects it. Many of our students come with a clear idea of what they want to do, and others figure it out during the program. At IESE Business School, about 40 percent of our full-time MBA students say they are doing the program in order to make a fundamental change in their careers.

The last, and in my view, best reason to do an MBA, or any master's degree, is to broaden your perspective and develop your own personal frameworks with which to understand the field you are interested in.

One of the most common reasons to not do the MBA or to put it off is to feel that it is too expensive. The good news is that there is a wide variety of programs at different price points and also a number of scholarships and loans available.

Another reason to not do a master's is not having the time due to personal or professional commitments. This issue can, however, be managed to some degree by taking one of the many part-time programs available. If you need to keep working in order to pay the bills and your school fees, then part-time programs will make the most sense.

If you have the time and can find the money, the advantages of a full-time program have to do with being able to fully focus on both the academic and social aspects of the program. Full immersion not only is a good way to learn but also offers a real break from going to work every day, and many people remember their time at graduate school as a very special time in their life.

Full-time MBAs can also be done in one or two years. I believe the two-year option is particularly good for people who are still figuring out what they want to do.

The best reason not to do a master's is if you have no genuine interest in the subject matter. From time to time I have students who are doing an MBA but are not interested in business. Normally, such people come for other reasons such as family pressure, a chance to come to a nice city, having access to financing, and so on.

If you do not see your interest clearly, my advice is to delay an MBA until such an interest develops or perhaps do a master's degree in something else which is closer to your heart.

This last point raises the question of when the right time is to do a master's. I believe there are essentially two ideas to consider: the amount of work experience you already have and your personal situation.

If you have been working in a *space* for two years or so, you may have already decided that it is not right for you. In this case, going back to school is an accepted way out.

If, on the other hand, you have been working in the space for five years or more, then you are probably happy in it and feel you belong there. Although it is still possible to change course, you might choose to do an MBA to move faster through the ranks.

If you have 10–20 years of business experience, you may be drawn to do an MBA because you feel a need to learn. You may not even know exactly what that is but have a sense that you are "missing something."

Another question is where to go. These days there are excellent programs all over the world, from Chicago to Shanghai and from Boston to Barcelona. All of the leading schools have qualified faculty, teach similar subjects and sometimes even use the same case studies and simulations.

In terms of the potential for personal transformation, there is a lot to gain by being surrounded by people who are very different than yourself and living in a new place outside of your comfort zone.

On the other hand, if it is already clear that your future is in the North American Automotive Industry and your hope is to be able to live near friends and family in Michigan, then going to business school at Ann Arbor or Wayne State might be the best decision because those schools are well-known to the people in that *space*.

The last question to look at is to choose a school which is focused on a specific area such as finance or one which is more generalist. All schools will do a good job in all subjects, but there are institutions which are known for specific things. They tend to attract the very best faculty in those areas and also have the most well-connected alumni networks in the same fields. Naturally companies in those fields like to recruit their students.

Perhaps the least important thing to look at is where is a particular school in the different rankings published by newspapers, magazines and websites. In general, I am skeptical about the accuracy of most of these rankings but do agree that there is an elite group of schools at the top which one might want to consider.

These schools tend to benefit from a certain circular logic as they attract fantastic students who go on to do amazing things in the world. As the reputation grows, so does the caliber of the students and so on.

Adult education

If you feel you need to learn more about a topic but either do not have the time to pursue a degree or already have one, nondegree programs might be the right solution. Again, the type of such programs I know best are the ones offered at business schools, and these are typically called "executive education."

Most business schools offer a portfolio of such courses which can be as short as two days or as long as six to nine weeks or months.

The shorter programs are terrific in getting a deep dive into specific topics. These topics are usually timeless issues such as increasing financial acumen or hot topics like how to understand and apply AI.

Longer programs typically cover many of the same issues as an MBA but do so to a lesser degree of depth and are targeted at people with more work experience. In such a program you will be given a window on the most critical areas of modern management thought, finance, operations, globalization, marketing, human resources, and so on.

The conceptual difference between these programs and the MBA is that in the MBA you do not just get to look through a window on such topics but actually are thrown out the window and into the conceptual snow.

Typically, MBA programs and other rigorous master's programs do not let students graduate unless they achieve a reasonable level of competence.

As opposed to an MBA (or other master's programs), which is accredited by international bodies, executive education programs usually give credentials which are subject only to the school's own criteria, and usually one will pass the course by simply being present and paying attention.

In specific *places* and *spaces*, however, such credentials do have significant market value and are highly thought of. A number of business schools, for example, offer a portfolio of long management programs which are targeted at different types of *roles* in a typical company.

Wherever you live, it is likely that there is a leading school in the area that offers such programs either in business or in other disciplines such as project management, health care administration, executive coaching or whatever you are interested in.

As will be discussed, the key issues to look at in choosing such programs is if the content will give you the training you need, if you can afford the cost of the program in terms of time and money and what kind of reputation does the program have in terms of its value in the relevant market.

Online Learning

Since its invention in 1989 by Tim Berners-Lee, the World Wide Web has expanded exponentially. By the end of 2020, one estimate gave the total number of active websites around the world to be about 400 million. The web houses pretty much all of human knowledge in one form or another.

Starting in the early 2000s a number of digital learning platforms began to take shape in order to harness that knowledge and get it out to people. The issue has attracted entrepreneurs, philanthropists and also traditional universities.

By the time the pandemic hit in 2020, online learning had become effective at delivering content but not so good at fostering the kind of interaction between people that is the hallmark of learning face to face.

The massive online open course or Mooc became fashionable in the early 2000s, and at one time it looked like the university's days might be numbered. Silicon Valley threw money and technology at the issue and a number of start-ups emerged to capture what some people called EdTech.

When they first came out, some Moocs were being attended by tens of thousands of students at a time. The basic idea of the Mooc is that a teacher can extend their reach across many more students than by confining themselves to a lecture hall.

In its noblest articulation, organizations such as Khan Academy strive to democratize knowledge and empower millions of people around the world regardless of where they live, who they are or how much money they have.

Another part of the online story is how traditional distance-learning organizations, such as London's Open University, adopted the new technology to make themselves even more relevant than they had been in the past. Other schools, such as St. Louis University, went all in on e-learning and now offer a full range of accredited degrees and have hundreds of thousands of students.

Part of the challenge of online learning is that the technology, industry and business model is still evolving. The issues are all about how to reach the most people with a specific platform or course, on the one hand, and how to give them the most meaningful and credible experience on the other.

Online learning, however, jumped ahead during the pandemic as most schools were forced to go online as a result of the lockdowns and travel restrictions. At our school we had no choice other than to teach our programs on line for a number of months and then move to a hybrid format with some students online if they could not come to class.

The most compelling types of online courses which I am familiar offer specific technical skills such as coding or maintenance of sophisticated machinery. Increasingly such courses can help make the transition from one kind of *role* to another and many have a proven track record in terms of job placement in either the full-time or gig economy.

As mentioned earlier, however, the technology will continue to improve, and we will eventually see fully immersive virtual classrooms, like that seen in Steven Spielberg's *Ready Player One* and Ernest Cline's book with the same title on which it was based. Meta, the company that manages facebook and other social media platforms is fully committed to building out the metaverse to enable this type of education as well as other offerings.

Beyond Business

Because I teach in a business school, I have used examples from my own experience to illustrate the key differences between different types of education. There are, however, many things that are taught in a variety of programs around the world. As I think about the future and some of the key trends and issues that we already know are coming, I would highlight the following 10 areas of potential study.

Please do not be concerned if you do not see your own chosen area of interest in my top 10. These areas I have chosen based on what I see in the business world, and they are closely related to the lists of *spaces* and *roles* presented in chapters 4 and 5.

Besides the learning involved, getting a certificate or some other qualification from a reputable training school may increase your employability in the different *spaces* associated with these topics.

1) Artificial Intelligence

AI has to do with developing algorithms so that computers can make a recommend decisions based on crunching through enormous quantities of information. Most experts in this field, like my colleague Samsa Samila, believe AI to be a general-purpose technology like electricity. Such technologies are remarkable because their use quickly spreads across the global economy and transforms the way things are done.

Having a working knowledge of how this technology works and could be deployed will be important in many of the *spaces* that will dominate the future including health care, energy and commerce.

In this field you might want to look at the applications side of AI meaning what you can do with it or the data science which is about how to build the data sets and design the algorithms.

2) Cybersecurity

Cybersecurity is a range of technologies that procedures which make the digital infrastructure of the world safe. It includes the systems and communications architecture as well as physical security without which the digital world will be vulnerable to attacks by criminals, terrorists and geopolitical rivals.

Many degree programs in information technology offer courses and concentrations on cybersecurity, but there are also a number of online and face-to-face options to look into, although many require some prior knowledge of coding.

3) Energy

As discussed at length in Chapter 1, the world is in the process of moving toward a low carbon energy mix. Although this process will happen faster or slower depending on the politics of a specific *place*, the direction is clear and is opening up huge professional opportunities for people who understand how the new technologies work and how to deploy them.

Within the topic, there are many specific areas that could be studied such as particular energy sources including wind and different types of solar power, energy conservation technologies and a host of distribution issues.

One of the largest opportunities in this area is for technicians and operators as much of the work needed involves retrofitting buildings and infrastructure. While many people already have the needed experience with electrical, plumbing, insulation and other basic building blocks of the modern world, a better understanding of how the new devices work and are connected to each other will make it easier to become part of this coming boom.

4) Sustainability

Beyond energy, there are a number of topics associated with making the world more sustainable in terms of its environmental and social footprint. Sustainability is becoming important in all aspects of business including the design of products and services, purchasing, marketing and also taking responsibility for products at the end of their useful life. In addition to the business world, there are also opportunities in the public sector and non profit sector.

Sustainability also has both an environemntal and social side and some programs deal with one, the other or both of these topics.

5) Health care

Applications to nursing and medical schools have increased sharply as a result of the pandemic. In addition to traditional health care careers, there is also increasing demand at chiropractic colleges around the world as well as other therapeutic disciplines.

Besides clinical specialties, the digitalization of health care has opened the doors to a myriad of training opportunities for people in data science, instrumentation and the operation of all types of medical technology and devices.

A quick look at any of the leading schools will show a number of programs on a range of topics which range from short courses for doctors and nurses to master's degree in subject like "Applied Health Sciences Informatics" to literally dozens of specializations and PhDs.

What does characterize the health care training industry to some degree is a very close relationship to specific *roles* in the overall health care *space*. You can, for example, take a course in many places to become a cardiovascular technician, EMT, and so on.

6) Entertainment

The demand for gaming and entertainment will continue to increase over time. These *spaces* employ many different types of people, and like in health care, there are specialized schools and programs available for everything from acting and directing to operating equipment, developing special effects and producing digital art. The real question is what specific *role* and *space* you are interested in and then figure out what training and credentials you need to get into it.

One issue to consider in this and other creative industries is that training and education is often not enough to be successful. There is also some almost mystical combination of real talent, luck and connections that all need to come together if you are aiming for the top.

This is not to say that getting a solid education is not important in these fields, but rather only that it may not be enough to break into one of these *spaces*.

7) Politics and international relations

If you are intrigued by the major challenges facing the world, then you may be attracted to the study of international relations or public policy directly.

Probably the most interesting course I ever took was a weeklong program at Harvard's Kennedy School of Government.

There are a large number of schools all over the world which offer a mix of short-term and long-term programs as well as different types of degree programs. Perhaps the only caution I would give is that often such schools appear to have something of a political bias and you should be aware of these biases before going.

8) Science and technology

Besides digital technology and energy mentioned earlier, there are a number of scientific disciplines which will continue to remake the world we live in. Biotechnology, nanotechnology, aerospace, and so on are all fields exploding in terms of human knowledge.

There are a range of courses and programs available on all of these topics which could lead to different *roles*. These types of courses, however, do require real passion and commitment as well as a very solid technical background.

9) Languages

If you are planning to relocate to another part of the world or work for a company which has its headquarters in a different country, then taking language courses may be a good idea.

Learning to speak someone else's language not only is rewarding in and of itself but also gives you greater insight into how they think and shows your interest and commitment.

10) Humanities

My final recommendation is to consider studying humanities such as economics, history, literature or the arts, especially if you have studied engineering or some other very technical field in the past.

When I went to engineering school back in the 1980s, we had mandatory humanities credit every semester as it was thought that we will only be well-rounded people if we have read and studied world history and the classics.

Studying humanities later in life may not lead directly to a specific *space* or *role* but will increase your understanding of the human condition. If you never had the opportunity to obtain a college degree, this might be an interesting option to consider especially if you have a genuine interest in one of these topics.

How to Choose?

While I am convinced that all of us will need to undergo periodic training, your own needs are particular to your situation and will change at different times of your professional life. To help you sort through this complex maze, the following are a series of criteria with which to look at different options. These are by the way, given in chart J in chapter 12.

The first thing to look at is the institution offering the course. Check out its reputation and place in the rankings both at the global level and in the specific *space* and *place* you are interested in. I call this "aspect portability," meaning a title from this institution is widely recognized.

Next describe the course in the terms that are most relevant. Is it, for example, full time or part-time, face to face or online or blended? My suggestion is to list the items that will be most important in comparing one opportunity to another.

The next question is how much the program will cost you in terms of tuition, travel and living expenses, as well as the opportunity cost. Opportunity cost is the money you will not make if you have to leave your current position or reduce your hours in order to take the course.

One of the reasons that many people come to full-time programs during economic downturns is that their opportunity cost get close to zero since they don't have a job anyway.

Timeliness has to do with the extent the course is more about keeping up with a changing field such as block chain applications or more about timeless subjects like critical reasoning, finance or strategy. The importance of each one of these objectives will change for you at different points in your professional life.

Professional relevance is, in some ways, the opposite of timeliness and has to do with how focused a course or program is on the specific challenges associated with the work you want to be doing. It may be very direct such as robotics or 3D printing applied to a specific industry.

The last criteria is about your own style of learning since some people do better in a self-guided environment, while others will flourish in a cohort where everyone learns together at a standard pace.

The idea behind laying out educational alternatives in a clear way is to be able to help you compare very different options. The hope is to clearly articulate what is the underlying rationale for pursuing each course and then be able to choose between them.

Omni Learning and a Change in Mindset

The last idea in this chapter on education is the term coined by Evgeny Kaganer and Giuseppe Auricchio called *Omni Learning*. The idea is to use inter-active software tools to make every working day an opportunity to learn and to constantly track and update each employee's knowledge base, skill set and performance.

At the personal level, *Omni Learning* is about adopting a mindset and an attitude focused on lifetime learning. As the world becomes more complex and careers more varied, this idea will be of increasing importance since we will have to be constantly learning new things.

Omni Learning recognizes that most of what we learn in our professional work is essentially on the job. We figure things out by doing them and a good boss gives us feedback on our work so that we get better.

One formal approach to this idea was developed by the Center for Creative Leadership, a consulting company which says that 70 percent of an executive's development should happen via challenges and experiences on the job, 20 percent through feedback and coaching by other people and 10 percent in formal coursework. In their model the 10 percent acts as an amplifier of everything else.

The idea behind Omni Learning is to take that other 90 percent and systemically target what you are learning. Some companies, for example, have people rate the way a colleague facilitated a meeting in real time and provide direct feedback. That idea can then be connected to the development goals that the same person has.

The way the process was described to me is to develop a fit-bit for work.

Personally, I am a bit taken aback by the full digitalization of everything we do. I have a similar reaction to microobjectives and rewards which feel a bit intrusive to me.

I am, on the other hand, attracted by the idea of putting learning at the center of people management. One could, for example, see many interactions with staff as a "learning moment" and not wait till the annual performance review to give feedback.

Perhaps the biggest idea I take away from *Omni Learning* is the change in mindset that it invites you to adopt. If you see your professional life as a journey in learning, then everything you do becomes an opportunity.

As discussed earlier, the changing world will force you to go back to school or whatever mechanism or platform you choose. It will also, however, require you to do things you never did before and learn new concepts and techniques all the time.

What makes it all worthwhile in my view is to connect all of these experiences with your own idea of the larger purpose that you are trying to achieve and the values you hold. That is the topic of Chapter 11.

Key Ideas Chapter 10

- Given the pace of change, you will need to continue learning during your professional career.
- Formal educational programs can be done face to face and online, and some offer degrees while others do not.

- Online learning has improved and its use has increased sharply as a result of the pandemic.
- Regardless of your area of interest, a college degree is an important symbol in today's business world and should be considered.
- Masters programs and other educational options can be helpful when changing from one phase to another in your professional life.
- Besides business education, there are number of other fields which you might consider including
     1. AI
     2. Cybersecurity
     3. Energy
     4. Sustainability
     5. Health care
     6. Entertainment
     7. Politics and international relations
     8. Science and technology
     9. Langauges
    10. Humanities

CHAPTER 11

PURPOSE AND VALUES

Perhaps the most lasting impact of the pandemic and the war in Europe is that these events caused many people to realize the importance of aspects of our lives we may have been taking for granted such as health, family and friends. At the professional level, part of what may have drieven a rise in resignations during the pandemic was people asking themselves about the purpose of their lives.

You might be asking the same question in one way or another.

This chapter focuses on the issue of purpose in the hope of helping you reflect on what is most important to you. The discussion goes beyond the idea of finding the right combinations of *space*, *role* and *place* in order to help you connect with that larger purpose.

You, for example, might feel that there is a trade-off between purpose and fulfillment on one side and paying the bills on the other. Rather than see these two ideas as a zero-sum game, meaning and practicality are, in my view, like an equation. People who love what they do tend to do it well and can sometimes make more money because of that.

Another option is to find purpose outside of our professional lives and thus look for practical things like money and security when looking at professional choices. You may find purpose in working on the big problems of the world, raising a family, building community or perhaps doing what you believe to be God's will.

After six months of confinement, a colleague felt that she needed to be more present for her children who were going to school online and decided to quit her job. Fortunately, her husband was making enough money to make her choice possible, and not everyone has that option. She is convinced that she will get back to her professional life at some point in the future but felt that in the current state of things, it made more sense to focus on her children's education.

Man's Search for Meaning

Viktor Frankl was an Austrian psychiatrist who was working on his theory of human motivation when he was sent to a Nazi concentration camp in 1942. He not only managed to survive Auschwitz and three other concentration camps over the next four years but also made use of his experiences to formulate his idea that the fundamental drive for human existence is a search for meaning.

Frankl's idea was a stark departure from Freud, who argued that our primary purpose was seeking pleasure. For Frankl, meaning can come from three different sources. The first is doing things in the world and making a difference. This is the driver of the mission statements of many companies and organizations.

My business school, for example, has the mission to "develop leaders who will have a deep and lasting positive impact on themselves, their companies, and society." If the individuals who work in an organization make that purpose their own, they can derive true meaning from their work.

You have probably heard the story of US president John F. Kennedy asking a man cleaning a hallway at NASA's facility in Cape Canaveral, Florida, what he was doing. According to the story, the man replied that he was putting a man on the moon.

Another of Frankl's sources of meaning was passively appreciating nature, art or beauty, or the act of loving or caring for others. A relation of mine finally retired at 86 after a very successful career as a leading medical expert, doctor and health care administrator.

After his retirement, he and his wife moved across the country to live closer to his oldest son and his growing family. After the move, they were able to see more of their young grandchildren and also become avid patrons of the local cultural scene spending their evenings going to the theater, concerts and even the opera. The temporary suspension of these activities during 2020 was a heavy blow as they had built their new life around them.

The third source of meaning for Frankl, which seems to be driven by his horrific experience, is simply managing to keep one's head and survive a terrible ordeal with dignity and human values. Tens of millions have suffered loss and hardship as a result of the pandemic and such times are part of human existence. For Frankl, the question is how people confront those difficult times.

Frankl's view is that people who find meaning in their lives will be happy, useful members of society. His message is one of personal responsibility, as we all have a constant stream of decisions to take and through them decide if we are to live life as a scoundrel or in an effort to do the right thing to the best of our ability.

One of the ideas which struck me most in Frankl's account of his experiences is when he and his fellow inmates lose all of their belongings and are stripped naked as they begin their life in the camp. For these prisoners it did not matter who or what they were in their past life, and they only had their pure existence to draw upon.

Nina Simone, the great blues singer, sang a song called "I Got Life" which was written for the musical *Hair* and gets at the heart of the issue. After going through a long list of all the things that the singer did not have, the song turns to how the singer does have their body, dignity and life.

I see many people who have lost their jobs or positions and therefore their sense of self. Sometimes, they become depressed as they had built much of their personal identity around their chosen profession and their ability to make things happen.

This can be particularly hard on retired people if they have not developed a deep passion for something else such as family, local politics or a specific activity such as painting or woodworking. According to Frankl, purpose can be found in later stages of life by looking back on our deeds and accomplishments in the past, but I am, personally, not convinced that this will be enough for me.

In 2012, I watched an interview of Shimon Peres, the former president of Israel, which changed the direction with my professional life and has led, among other things, to my writing this book. Peres was at the World Economic Forum in Davos and was interviewed by Thomas Friedman, the author of *The World Is Flat*.

After a particularly insightful description of some of the issues facing the modern Middle East, Friedman was clearly impressed and asked Peres how he could still be himself at 93. He even asked him if his secret was eating a lot of yogurt. Peres's answer was that one had to compare the list of achievements that we have made in our life with the list of dreams we still had in our head. In his view, as long as the list of dreams was longer than the list of achievements, a person was still young.

After watching the interview, I realized that at the age of 50 I was stuck in a professional rut. I had been teaching the same course for over 15 years and was doing little to impact the world besides working with my own students. Since then, I have published four books, developed new courses and began to speak in public about issues that I believe are important.

For Frankl, the meaning of his life was to help people to find meaning in theirs. I invite you to think about your own life and what you think your own purpose has been and will be as a way to guide your thinking through the exercises and frameworks presented in this book.

Different Types of Meaning

The question of meaning becomes very important as you think about the trade-offs you might need to make between *space*, *role* and *place* as you go from job to job and phase to phase in your professional life. For many people the choice revolves around either finding purpose in their work or working in order to provide for themselves and their family and finding purpose in other parts of their life.

The heroes in Ayn Rand's novel, *Atlas Shrugged*, for example, were business leaders who built things. They created modern society through a combination of new technology, industrial organization and their own force of will.

You may find meaning by producing consumer products, cars, financial services and other such things. You might, on the other hand, see your role as making the world more efficient by introducing new technologies or business models.

A different approach is to find meaning in solving a specific problem as discussed in Chapter 4. This might be one of the large global problems such as helping the world prepare for the next pandemic, mitigate climate change or extend access to clean water and sanitation. Your challenge might also be a more local issue such as raising funds for a new sports facility or school library or building up a local church, mosque or synagogue.

My mother, for example, worked as a manager of meal programs for senior citizens in a medium-sized city and then moved to a much smaller town where she had lived before after officially retiring at 65.

There, she worked part-time in a series of jobs to supplement her pension but has also been very active in creating a local Jewish community, serving on the county's grand jury and raising money for a local homeless shelter. She not only found meaning through these endeavors but also created community around her which has given her tremendous joy and comfort during the difficult times during the pandemic.

You might find meaning in being with your family, pursuing a particular passion or coaching the local soccer or baseball team. The central idea is that the reason for going to work is to make enough money to do the things that are really important.

If this is the plan, then I urge you to make sure that the job or career chosen gives you enough time and energy left at the end of the day or the week to really be able to make that contribution in a satisfactory way. There were a number of years in my own life when I was working so hard that I lost track of important things like my relationship with my family and my own health and fitness.

Like my old job as a management consultant, many high-paying *roles* require dedication, significant travel, late nights and weekend work.

Many managers and executives fall into this trap and say to themselves that they are working hard "for their family" since such work can be financially rewarding. In my personal experience the money is fine but is typically spent on having more stuff, bigger houses and better cars. As discussed at length in Chapter 7, having more things does not necessarily make us happier people.

The other part of the story is that this type of work is also a bit addictive and even intoxicating. If you do it well, you are given constant praise and professional recognition.

What also happens is that all of your peers and colleagues are also doing similar things, and not only does it become normal but you might also feel that you cannot fall behind.

The main impact that the pandemic has had on these types of *roles* is that business travel has been sharply reduced or even eliminated and replaced with spending enormous amounts of time on Zoom, Teams or other platforms. A new problem is that in global businesses, these calls have ended up taking place at all hours of the day or night putting additional strain on family life.

The downside to this path is well described in *The Knight in the Rusty Armor*, a fable by Robert Fisher, which has sold millions of copies worldwide. The story is about a knight who spends so much time fighting dragons that he not only ruins his relationship with his wife and child but also ends up trapped inside his armor which has rusted shut. In the story, the knight lost track of why he was fighting dragons in the first place and became completely absorbed in the fight.

The book helped me realize some of the mistakes I made in my own life, and this is one of the reasons I place such importance on this discussion of purpose and meaning.

My interest in this discussion is not to tell you what is important to you but to encourage you to think about it. Do you feel a deep connection to the stated purpose of the organization that you are working for? Are you putting a man on the moon?

If not, do you have a clear idea of what the role of your professional work is in relation to the rest of your life and where you do find meaning? Is there enough balance in terms of time, money and energy so that you can actually put everything together in a way that is sustainable over time and will bring you meaning and joy?

Leading with Meaning

One of the things that I observed during the onset of the pandemic in the spring of 2020 was how different companies and their leaders reacted. Many seemed a bit lost and jumped from decision to decision in an ad hoc fashion.

Others were able to step back and use their own stated definitions of ideas like mission, vision and values to decide what was most important and acted accordingly. When times got very tough, I also saw how those organizations which had a mission which resonated with the men and women who worked in it were able to tap into that connection and accomplish extraordinary things. I see the same pattern as firms work out their reposnse to Russia's invasion of Ukraine.

Mission, vision and values

Two business school professors, David Collis and Michael Rukstad, developed definitions for the terms "vision," "mission," "values" and "strategy" which I use in my own executive education classes.[1]

For Collis and Rukstad, the *Mission* of an organization is the fundamental reason why it exists. Tesla, for example, says its mission is to "to accelerate the world's transition to sustainable energy." The fact that the company started out by making cars is actually only part of its story, and one can see how Tesla has made some extremely controversial decisions, such as buying Solar City, a company which installed solar panels, as a result of the pursuit of that mission.

The *Vision* is a statement indicating what the organization is striving to be *some day*. The key point is that *some day* is deliberately not well-defined and may take many years to accomplish. This is different than their definition of *Strategy* which has specific financial and operational targets as well as a well-defined period of time.

The last piece of Collis and Rukstad's framework is the statement concerning the *Values* that the men and women who make up the organization agree to adhere to in pursuit of the *Mission, Vision* and *Strategy*.

The idea is that there are limits to what can be done in pursuit of the mission and vision. Organizations with a strong values culture will not tolerate certain types of behavior. Values can go even further than compliance, which has to do with the letter of the law.

---

1   Collis, D.J. and Rukstad, M.G., 2008. Can you say what your strategy is?. Harvard business review, 86(4), pp.82–90.

A *Values Statement* typically discusses timeless ideas such as integrity, accountability, diversity, and so on. When taken seriously, in cases like Johnson & Johnson's famous credo, it can guide decision making at the strategic and operational level and serve to attract, motivate and retain the best people.

In some cases, however, values are often discounted as meaningless expressions of intention without true significance. The best way to see what is going on in a specific organization is to compare its stated values with the behavior of its senior people. If the people at the top are not walking the talk, then I would not put too much emphasis on the value statement even if it is written in big letters on the wall.

Going back to the first few months of the pandemic in the spring of 2020, it was very clear which companies really followed their stated values about employee well-being and safety and for which these were empty words.

Your values

Most of us are taught values by our parents and the community that we grew up in. A new statement about corporate values is often met with indifference, skepticism or even a degree of hostility if such statements are made with little or no cultural awareness or tact.

The point of this discussion of corporate values is to encourage you to reflect on your own values and to make sure that there is some degree of connection between your own sense of right and wrong and that of the organization that you choose to work for.

If for whatever reason you do not share the stated values of the company or organization you are a part of, then I would think about whether it is really the right place for you. A different issue is the degree to which the leaders of the organization live up to the values it says are important.

In some cases, values are, like the vision, something the organization is striving for, and it might make sense to be patient and support the gradual change in behavior that the leadership is committed to.

In others, there is a sharp disconnect between the stated values and what the organization actually does. In 2015 it was found that Volkswagen, for example, had deliberately manipulated the software in its diesel engines to give misleading pollution control readings putting into question its entire strategy of clean mobility and its integrity as a company. The scandal has cost the company approximately $20 billion in fines and payments to different stakeholders as well as the resignation of two CEOs and a number of other executives.

In another example, a large number of employees of Google were horrified to find that the company had quietly settled a sexual harassment case and generously pensioned off the alleged offender in order to avoid a trial and negative publicity. Google has a well-established code of conduct which covers 7 different categories and 33 specific areas including everything from conflicts to discrimination, harassment and bullying in any form.

Since its founding Google has been committed to the idea of "do no evil," and when employees saw a difference in what they understood that their company stood for and what it actually was doing, it created a huge crisis of conscience for many of them and a problem for management.

In search of purpose

Recognizing the importance of purpose, companies spend enormous time and energy in crafting and communicating their statements about their mission, vision and values. Often this effort is connected to the idea of corporate social responsibility (CSR) and a related concept which is the company's performance in terms of environment, social and governance (ESG) issues.

Over the last few years many firms have taken the time to publicly commit themselves to supporting specific examples of the United Nations Sustainable Development Goals (see Box 11) as a way of communicating what they stand for and why they are in business.

BOX 11: THE SUSTAINABLE DEVELOPMENT GOALS

The 2030 Agenda for Sustainable Development was adopted by all United Nations Member States in 2015. At its heart are the 17 Sustainable Development Goals (SDGs) which replaced the UN's millennium Development Goals which guided international humanitarian efforts between their adoption in 2000 and 2015.

The 17 goals, and the 169 targets in which they are broken down, cover a range of topics including ending poverty and hunger, providing water and sanitation, promoting gender equality, and of course tackling the problems associated with the environment including air and water pollution and climate change.

The good news is that by the end of 2019, many countries had made significant progress towards reaching the goals largely as a result of hundreds of millions of people moving into the global economy in the developing world. The bad news is that the global pandemic has hit these same developing countries very hard and has set back the development agenda by 5–10 years.

What many leading companies are doing is to explicitly link their own sustainability and broader Corporate Social Responsibility agenda to the 17 goals and their more specific targets. Most companies that do this have selected the 4–6 SDGs that they feel are particularly relevant given their line of business, geographic location and the specific concerns of their customers, employees, shareholders and other stakeholders.

Finally, the goals also offer an opportunity for individuals who want to link their professional lives with a broader, perhaps more meaningful social purpose. Connecting your own professional ambitions to one of the goals is an interesting way to define the *space* you want to look at and will also make a compelling story to tell contacts and potential employers.

The Coca-Cola Company, for example, has managed to make its operations water neutral (goal number 7) in 2015—investing to first save and then replace the fresh water that it uses in its products and operations. Coke has been actually working on the water issue since the early 2000s due to problems it caused in water supply to some villages in India. Coke is currently working to become waste neutral by 2030 contributing to goal number 12.

While much of this effort is about rebranding and communicating things that the company already does, I do see value in using the SDGs as a common language to discuss issues of purpose and meaning, when the initiatives are real.

A cynical view is that the only reason companies are spending time and energy on environmental and social issues is because the financial community has started paying attention to these issues. Whatever the reason, you may find such activity by the company you work for motivating.

Compromises and Phases

A question I am often asked is if it is okay to compromise and spend significant time and energy working for an organization in which one has little or no resonance in terms of meaning and purpose. There can be no clear-cut answer to the question as everyone's situation is unique, and the answer may change at different points in your life.

Compromises

Overall, however, I feel that you should avoid situations in which what you care about and what the organization or company you work for are doing are completely at odds. If, for example, you are passionate about addressing the issue of climate change, then perhaps there are some companies you might avoid working for.

Where this gets tricky is in the details and shades of gray. You might, for example, say that anyone who cares about the environment should not work for the major oil companies as their product contributed directly to the problem. On the other hand, the facts are that Exxon Mobil spends hundreds of millions of dollars on research into new types of energy, and working in that effort could be an opportunity to really make a difference.

A former student faced a similar situation when she was the chief sustainability officer for a chain of supermarkets which sold enormous quantities of produce in plastic packaging. Her feeling was that she could have a more positive impact by reducing the footprint of the chain and that of its customers than by criticizing the company from the outside. Such choices are deeply personal, and you need to decide your own path.

Questions like these get at the heart of the question of purpose. In some cases the answers are relatively easy and in others they are complex and subtle.

One rule of thumb which might be helpful is that if you cannot explain what your company does to an eight-year-old in positive terms, then perhaps it is the wrong place for you.

Changes over time

People in their 20s tend to look ahead to the world of work with positive energy and ambition. Most will tell me that they want to "make a difference" and will be choosy about the companies and organizations with which they get involved.

I have come to the conviction that most important thing to do in the first phase of your professional life is to decide what overall direction you should start out on and also what direction not to take. After that, the key is to make sure that each job or step brings sufficient learning and experience in order to set up the next one. Try to avoid big mistakes, but if they do happen, learn from them and move on.

At some point during these early years I think it is very important to learn a set of skills and become good at doing a *role* or understanding the ins and outs of a specific *space*. The model that is often talked about for professional development is to use the letter T, which had a long vertical part supporting a horizontal top.

Applying this to professionals, it is helpful to develop depth in a specific area—perhaps in your late 20s and/or early 30s in order to build across different areas as you move up in the different departments or organizations where we work. During this phase I strongly recommend doing something for which you have some basic affinity for the *space* itself and some natural inclination for the *role* you play.

If your life follows a conventional path, at some point, you may find yourself living with another person and perhaps having a family to support. You may also balance your professional life with commitments to civic and political organizations, sports, and so on. It is often necessary to make more compromises at this phase than before.

You may, for example, be asked to relocate far from friends and your greater family network and have to deal with the issues such relocation can create for your family as a whole.

You may also find yourself working with people you do not particularly like. As discussed in Chapter 8, there are moments when the only thing to do is to quit. There are, however, others when the situation is not that bad, and the right choice is to set aside your ego and pride and keep your job and situation secure. Again this is a very personal choice and depends completely on the actual situation.

After some period of time, you might find yourself choosing between management or becoming more of a subject matter expert. Some organizations have well-developed career tracks for such experts, although many still give more money and recognition to people who manage larger parts of the business. The compromise that many managers are forced to make at this stage is to lose contact with their clients, patients or products and join the ranks of the "suits" who run things.

My one piece of advice if this is happening to you is to make sure you have a full understanding of the financial issues involved in your work as finance is the language of business. Every business school offers, by the way, short courses on finance for business managers.

As you move up the ranks, I think it is even more critical to have a feeling or even a passion for the business as I think it is difficult to lead others if you do not believe in the mission of the organization. Such affinity is particularly important for entrepreneurs who need to get their investors, employees and customers to share in their vision.

As I get older, I am increasingly in contact with colleagues and friends who are approaching the end of their classic career and moving into some intermediate stage between a fully demanding career and retirement in the fullest sense of the word.

If you are moving into this phase of your professional life, you may focus on a combination of doing interesting projects, advising others and doing things which might have a greater social purpose such as volunteer work or community service. One last aspect of this later phase in life is to make sure that you set up the last phase or what might be called the endgame for lack of a better description.

The Spanish poet Machado once wrote that "the road is made by walking along," and while I believe there is a lot of truth to the idea, I also think having an idea of where we want to go is a very useful.

For you, the destination might consist of a house near the beach and maybe a sailboat in a *place* with a nice climate. On the other hand, it might be farmhouse with a large vegetable garden or a condo in a gated community with a championship golf course.

Different people understand leisure differently, and I think each one of us should at least be aware of what makes us happy in terms of where we live and some of the basic aspects of that life. A close friend actually moved back to the beach near Newcastle where he grew up, and while he could easily move to a warmer place such as Spain, there is something about being in the North of England that appeals to him in a powerful way.

A couple I know has set up their chiropractic office in the little French village where one of them had grown up and spends their free time fixing up the old farmhouse they live and work in.

The father of a friend of mine sold his architectural studio in his early 50s and spent the next 20 years sailing his wooden sailboat several times around the world.

I believe all of us should give some thought to what we would like to spend our time on when we have the chance to choose. The danger if we do not do this is we find ourself suddenly retired in the classic sense of the word with no clear idea of what to do with ourselves.

Not being able to fulfil a specific dream, such as walking the Appalachian trail, making the pilgrimage to Santiago de Compostela or sailing around the world is really a shame if it could have been achieved.

Get back on course

The pandemic and its broader impact has set many people off of their chosen path, and this may have happened to you. You may also have been personally impacted by the war in Ukraine and you find yourself in a new country. Because of the situation you may have had to take a temporary gig such as driving for one of the ride hailing services or doing some other kind of project work.

All of us will need to do some things in the course of our career simply because they are necessary. I would not suggest, however, that just because you had to take a detour, you should necessarily change your overall direction in terms of finding purpose and meaning.

Key Ideas Chapter 11

- Our professional life can be far more enriching if you can find meaning and purpose in it.
- Work may also be the way to have the means to find meaning in other aspects of your life but take care that it does not absorb all of your time and energy.

- The best companies and managers manage to foster the connection between work and purpose.
- What gives you meaning may change at different points in your career as will be your willingness to compromise.
- Critical events such as the pandemic may have forced you to go back a step or two, but I encourage you to get back on track and seek the best path forward for you and your family.

CHAPTER 12

CONCLUSION: MAKING IT HAPPEN

Years ago, a very successful metaphor for career planning was to choose the color of the parachute that you would use. The idea was that every person should figure out what they really desire and then to pursue that dream.

I believe a better description of what career management is like in the today's world is learning to fly. A person accelerates for about 12 seconds after jumping out of an airplane before reaching terminal velocity or 120 mph. In free fall, a skydiver needs to keep their cool and control their movements with great care as a wrong move can send them hurtling in the wrong direction or even cause them to spin out of control.

With skill and practice they can control their direction during their descent, link up with others and push themselves to their limits. What they cannot do during a jump is to stop, take a break and ignore the fact that they are falling toward the ground.

Like the skydiver in free fall, professionals need to keep calm and control their movements as change continues to accelerate in today's business environment.

Tracking is what skydivers call moving horizontally at the same time as falling through the air. In the late 1990s, several enthusiasts began developing skydiving suits with fabric between the legs and the arms that made the skydiver resemble a flying squirrel. Over the last 20 years, these suits have evolved into what are now called wingsuits.

Wingsuits fill up with air during a jump. This increases drag, slowing a skydiver's speed, and also gives lift because of the way they are shaped. They are the most popular choice for BASE jumpers. BASE is an acronym for building; antenna; span, meaning bridges; or earth, such as cliffs or a mountain. Using wingsuits, BASE jumpers can fly long distances or streak over the ground at high speeds in what is known as proximity flying.

To take the metaphor a little bit further, what is really needed in this very complex world is to have a winged suit to manage your professional life.

This way you could fly around obstacles, handle sudden gusts of wind and be able to really control the direction and speed of your professional development.

This last chapter of this book is about what you can do to get control of your professional life and accelerate your progress. The three areas which I think are critical in this endeavor are sorting through the tremendous amount of information that is available, getting advice along the way and writing everything down.

Scouting the terrain

Before jumping off a cliff, BASE jumpers do extensive research about the jump they are about to make and often use sophisticated digital tools to model their descent. They need to understand the contours of the ground, wind patterns and even evaluate the color of the rocks to estimate how much heat will be coming off of them during a jump. Warm ground causes the air above it to rise.

In thinking about what to do in the next part of your professional life, doing a similarly thorough analysis is absolutely essential. While there is some brief discussion of different *spaces* and *roles* in earlier chapters, it is not possible to give you, and every other reader, all of the information and perspectives you might need to make the right choice.

Have you ever seen one of the movies where the hero is obsessed to uncover the conspiracy that has affected them or their family? Typically, they are an ex-police officer, a journalist or an average person who is out to uncover the plot. They often use their kitchen or bedroom wall to represent all of the myriad connections between the different people, organizations and events they are trying to piece together. As they find new pieces of the puzzle, they will draw a connection between pictures or names.

What I am suggesting is that you take a similar approach to thinking about your professional future. In this effort you can start with *space, role* or *place* but should include doing your homework on all three.

Sources of information

The internet can offer you enormous quantities of information. The problem is that to be effective in the online environment you need to know enough about a topic to even know what to look for. A related but different challenge is to be in a position to determine if a specific data point is even true. The problem with the web is that it is also plagued by incomplete conclusions, distortions of reality and fake news.

To gain general knowledge of a topic, my advice is that you start by going to a more classic source of information, that is, books. The advantage of books is that they are written by authors or published by authorities that you can evaluate independently in terms of their trustworthiness. On any topic you will find a number of authors and specialists and often one source will reference additional ones in its bibliography.

You may then drill down further by looking at general or specialized media again focusing on those sources you think are reliable.

Once you have done some basic reading, the internet can fill in the gaps. Wikipedia and other sources do their best to provide unbiased and accurate information but are only as good as the sources that they rely on. One technique I find effective is to go back and forth between sources for Wikipedia articles and further digging on the internet searching for key words, and so on.

If you have the patience for it, there is also a rich universe of academic articles written about most things that again provide well-documented sources which you can then trace back to find the most influential authors on a given topic.

Typically, the more you learn, the deeper you will go into something. What makes it especially challenging is that the deeper you go the more you realize there is to learn.

When you are ready, there is no substitute for talking with people in the *role*, *space* or *place* you are interested in. Talking with people may, in fact, be the only way to really get a glimpse of things which are only emerging in the current new normal.

My advice, however, is to do some desk research before speaking to experts in order to make sure that you ask good questions and demonstrate your interest in a specific topic. These people may point you in different directions which will again require you to circle back, read a recommended book or go online to dig deeper into something.

Social scientists find that when they talk to enough people, they begin to get the same answers over and over. This is called statistical saturation, and I would urge you stop your data collection when you get to this point.

The last generic source of information is direct experience. A cousin of mine was once thinking about getting into the business of importing and exporting cheese. He found a way to work every Saturday for about a year at the cheese counter of an upmarket delicatessen. While the part-time job paid very little, he found the experience invaluable in terms of learning more about the product he loved.

Our full-time MBA students take the summer between their first and second years to work for a few months. My advice to them is always to use that time to fully explore a *role*, *space* or *place* that they may be thinking of going to after graduation. The large banks and consulting companies use these summer jobs as a way of screening candidates.

In addition to these basic ideas, the following will provide some specific recommendations on how to learn more about a *spaces*, *roles* and *places*.

Scouting the space

In any particular *space* things can get pretty technical pretty fast, and you may have to ease your way into the jargon and data that the people in that *space* normally use before you can even understand the articles and posts you will see on specialized websites and magazines.

What makes things even more complicated is the fact that any particular *space* may have a number of more classically defined industries or subsectors intersecting with it. This means, for example, if you are interested in the business of charging electric vehicles you may have to combine articles found in *Automotive News*, which is published in Detroit, with something from Powermag, which focuses on utilities.

Academic articles concerning *space* will most likely either talk about the technology involved or trends in the industry. The problem with looking at trends in academic journals is they typically lag the industry practice by a few years and are usually heavy on complex statistics. Many academicians, however, also publish books targeted at a wider audience, but these will likely paint a picture of the industry as it was some years ago.

As you come up to speed, then you can start to talk to people in the *space* using the active networking approach described in Chapter 9.

Scouting the role

Perhaps the first step in exploring a new role is to find out if such a *role* really exists and be sure about what it is called in a specific *space* or *place*. You might be able to find ideas on LinkedIn, Glassdoor and job sites such as Indeed.

To learn more about a specific *role* that you have identified, either read what someone who has done it has written about their experience, talk to people who are in that *role* or try it out yourself if you can.

The only thing to watch out for in the books is that such works tend to tell the author's own story and may not be very objective.

People love to talk about what they do especially when they are passionate about it. If you talk with several of them, you might get a sense of what these people tend to be like and if you can imagine yourself in their shoes. They will also be able to tell you how the *role* has changed as a result of the pandemic.

If you can arrange to shadow someone or even better to assist them in the *role* for a period of time, this might be the best source of information of all, although it may be difficult to arrange.

Scouting the place

In terms of *place*, there are essentially two questions to ask. One is what does the industrial fabric of the *place* or *places* you are interested in look like? The other is what is it like to live and work there?

The first question is which *spaces* are growing in that *place*. Every region and city has a website with a wealth of economic information as well as a chamber of commerce or other government agency which can give data on the local economy.

Once you know what to look for, local newspapers and the specialized press can fill in the blanks. Local entrepreneurs and business leaders will have given interviews at one time or another or recorded videos about what their companies are doing.

With this kind of information already in your head, you will then be ready to talk to people in the area to see which firms specifically are thought to be up and coming.

The second question is more about the quality of life you can expect to have in that *place*. How is this *place* tied to your immediate and extended family and web of relationships? Is it the right *place* for you in this phase of your life in terms of schools, housing, access to nature, culture and nightlife? What is the health care system like, and how has it gotten through these difficult times?

Desk research can take you pretty far, and data is provided by local government, schools and housing developments and also a variety of community and faith-based organizations which can give you insight in what it is actually like to live there.

The idea behind LinkedIn is that all of us are connected by just a few degrees to everyone else in the world. Using this technique, you should be able to find some people who are somehow connected to you who live in that *place* and can tell you more about it.

Finally, as travel restrictions are easing off, you can probably get to any part of the planet for a reasonable amount of money and choose to spend a few days or a part of your next vacation in a *place* of interest. Some friends of mine did just that and went to several cities over the course of a couple of years before choosing to move to Brighton, about an hour south of London.

Getting Advice

Base Jumpers make it a point to talk to as many people as they can who have made a jump they are planning to do, especially when flying over mountainous terrain. Such people may have insights into the wind speeds, thermals and things to watch out for. In thinking about what to do with your professional life, the same principal applies and is absolutely invaluable.

In general, the idea of going to other people for advice in business is the heart of what is normally called mentoring. Research shows that having a mentor will give you better career progression, faster promotions and higher pay as well as softer ideas like a higher sense of professional achievement.[1]

The traditional definition of a mentor is a more senior person who takes an interest in your professional development and career. A broader view is to look all of the people who may be able to give you advice about your professional development including peers, family members and people outside of the organization.

If you are looking to make substantial changes in terms of *space, role* or *place*, then you will want to cultivate a broader network of such advisers. If all of the people you go to for advice, for example, come from the same organization or *space*, then they will probably tell you similar things as their experiences will be similar.

Although the pandemic has made most people more open to having video conversations, developing such relationships requires time, energy and tact. In general, you should prepare well for such meetings but then be very humble about anything you think you know about a company or the *space* it operates in. You should also be clear about what you want to talk about and why.

The best results come when you are recommended by a trusted third party who tells the person you want to talk to that they should meet with you because you have an interesting point of view about something of interest to them. The

---

1   Monica Higgins and Kathy Kram, "Reconceptualizing Mentoring at Work: A Developmental Network Perspective." *Academy of Management Review* 26 (2001): 264–288.

key is to do enough desk research and other interactions so you really develop some interesting ideas.

I call this the content paradigm of connection which is very different than just asking someone to talk to one of your contacts as a personal favor. If you do have a good meeting with someone, then you can try and build on that relationship by asking them if you can come back in 3–12 months to let them know how you are doing. If possible, offer to buy them lunch or a coffee.

BOX 12: FLYING IN FORMATION

Working with others, either in loose informal networks, or in new forms of matrix or agile organizations is the new normal. Are you part of such a team? Are there people that you have worked with whom you feel a special affinity and would like to keep working?

Many years ago I was working for a large consulting company which had different industry groups including aerospace, health care, automotive, and so on. I was in the automotive group.

One day we came into the office to find that 21 out of 22 members of the aerospace practice resigned on the same day and went to a rival firm. You can imagine what the only person who was not invited to leave felt like!

This idea is particular important if you work in a series of projects, rather than for one specific company. Film people, for example, routinely work together on a number of projects over the years. In a similar way, a number of startups have kept the team largely intact even as they pivot the business or even start a new company in a different *space*.

A former colleague, Marco Tortoriello, is a professor at Bocconi Business School in Milan. He lectures about an idea he calls *organizational residue* or what people remember about you after you leave a *role* or an organization.

Professor Tortoriello would say that years later, no one will remember if you made your budget or not. What they will remember is whether you were competent, generous with your time, and treated others with respect.

Are there people who you have been working with at different times in your professional life and perhaps even at different companies? Are there people from your past who are doing interesting things and with whom you might want to reconnect?

Writing It Down

Attached is an appendix with a series of charts that are intended to assist you in developing the ideas laid out in this book. Writing your thoughts down on paper is a way of making them real and tangible. You may also find you can share some of the charts with members of your family or wider circle and get their input.

Personal inventory

The first worksheet is designed to help you articulate your experience, constraints and passion. The worksheet tracks the discussion in Chapter 2 on these different parts of the overall framework and asks you to list the different elements and make some notes or reflections about them.

Experience starts with which *spaces* you have worked in but feel free to list sectors or industries or whatever else you feel is most useful to you. You may find the section on passion challenging but do make the effort to think about what you really enjoy in terms of products, services or something else. On the section of constraints, I recommend that you work this out together with your life partner, if you have one, and perhaps even a wider circle of friends and family.

A. Personal Inventory

Experience	Reflection
Spaces	
Communities	
Countries & Regions - Lived in - Visited - Studied	
Languages - Mother tongue - Fluent - Conversational	
Skills - Expert - Capable - Not hopeless	
Style - Leadership - Followership	
Crucible Moments - Professional - Personal	

Passion	Personal Reflection
Products	
Services	
Personal Interests (Perhaps in teens)	
Other Sources of Deep Satisfaction	

Constraints	Personal Reflection
Annual or Monthly Expenditures	
Ethical Lines	
Family Issues	
Other Geographic Limitations	
Limitations on the Type of Firm	
Limitations on the Working Environment	

Your story

The next worksheet is meant as a guide for crafting your personal story. The guide has a section for each of the two metaphors explained in Chapter 3 since I find some people respond better to one than the other. In the reflection space, don't skip over your mistakes but do show how you have learned from them.

Once that is done move on to construct your story. For each phase or job discuss why you did it, what you learned and achieved and why you felt it was time to move on.

B. Your Story

Phase/Job	Story Line

The River	Reflection
First Job Story	
Progression from stage to stage	
Rapids or Calm Waters	
Capsizes	
Portage	

The Race	Reflection
The Field	
The Rough	
The Edge of the Forest	
The Forest	
The Swamp	
The Beach	

First ideas

This chart is designed to capture your first impressions concerning *space*, *role* and *place*. There are additional charts for each of the three aspects, but you should get some ideas on paper as soon as possible.

Remember that the idea of *space* goes beyond industry or sector. The key thing about a *space* is that you need to be able to clearly describe it and explain why you are attracted to it.

The idea of *role* goes beyond that of a job title or specific position. The two questions concerning role at this stage are, why you think you will like the *role* and why you think you will be good at it?

The third part of the chart has to do with *place* or where you want to live and work.

C. First Ideas

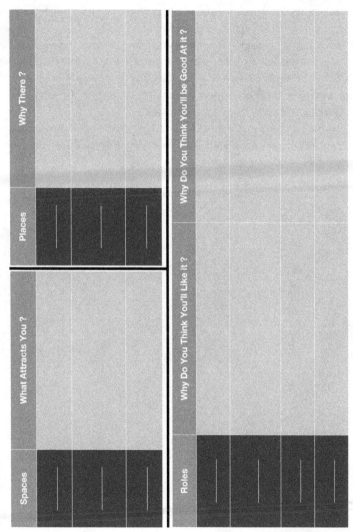

Spaces	What Attracts You ?	Places	Why There ?

Roles	Why Do You Think You'll Like it ?		Why Do You Think You'll be Good At it ?

Scenario development

In my view, the future is uncertain by definition, and each one of us has the ability and even the responsibility to chart a path for our professional future based on our assumptions and guesses about what the future might look like. You might paint two or possibly three different scenarios.

The chart gives some guidance and starts off with asking you what the time frame of your scenarios is. I suggest 15–20 years, but it is up to you. The next step is to look at the four trends discussed in Chapter 1 and any others you feel are important and think about how they might evolve. The last step is to combine the trends in some way that makes sense.

If you have a group of friends or like-minded people around you, then you may want to do this exercise with them as it will be fun and informative and you will get a better result by working with others.

D. Scenario Development

Time Horizon

Write down the year for which the future scenarios will be developed. Farther than the business cycle but soon enough to avoid science fiction. (e.g.15, 20, 25 years)

Drivers	Range of Outcomes
The Natural Environment	
Geo-Politics	
Digitalization	
Health and Well Being	

	Detailed Description & Narrative
Scenario 1	
Scenario 2	
Scenario 3	

Testing the space, role *and* place

The next three charts (E1, E2 and E3) are designed to help you see how the scenarios you have created will impact the *spaces*, *roles* and *places* you are interested in. Each chart is a little different, but all three are designed to see how your different choices may evolve over whatever time frame you choose to use.

Using the charts, you should be able to give an overall rating to each part of the framework, and I suggest color coding them as very positive (green), uncertain (yellow) or perhaps in deep trouble (red).

E1. Space Analysis

Ideas for Space
Ecosystem List the types of companies or organizations that are currently involved in the space and indicate which ones have the most weight or influence.
Issues or Problems List the issues or problems that the people and companies in this space are working to solve
Scenario Impact -1 Think through how the space might evolve in the case that the first scenario you envisioned in were to unfold. the third scenario you
Scenario Impact -2 Think through how the space might evolve in the case that the second scenario you envisioned in were to unfold.
Overall Evaluation - Green - Yellow - Red

E2. Role Analysis

	Role 1	Role 2	Role 3
Value Analysis Detail to what degree the service performed is considered higher or lower value in today's economy i.e. < $50 /Hour Between $50 and $150/Hr > $ 150/Hr			
Task Breakdown List the 3-5 key tasks that make up a specific. job or position			
Task Analysis (How important? from 1 - 5) • Complex Perception • Complex Manipulation • Creative Content • Social Intelligence			
Overall Evaluation - Green - Yellow - Red			

E3. Place Analysis

Ideas for Place				
Location & Region *Describe the place you are considering and in which country or city it is located*				
Attraction What is about the place that draws you such as: - Professional opportunity - Family & Friends - Climate / Lifestyle				
Tradeoffs What are the drawbacks to the location which could give you pause before committing to it?				
Environmental Issues How might the *place* might evolve in terms of quality of life, pollution and climate change				
Geo-political issues How might the *place* might evolve in terms of local, national and international political issues				
Health Issues To what degree is the *place* likely to be a center for innovation in digital, life sciences, energy, etc.				
Overall Evaluation - Green - Yellow - Red				

Combinations

Having gone through the analysis of your different ideas of *space*, *role* and *place*, the next chart gives you a place to write down the best combinations. This is where a combination of creativity, ambition and reality all come into play.

The challenge is creating a couple of combinations which will allow you to be part of a *space* that you feel deserves your time and energy at the same time as playing a *role* in which you will add value and be able to live and work in a *place* or you want to be.

The most difficult part of filling out this chart may be in crafting a description of the combination that you feel excited about. Share it with friends or people whose opinion you value.

F. Combinations

Alternative	Space	Role	Place	Detailed Description
1				
2				
3				

Happiness

The next chart is designed to help you make a choice between the different combinations by going through the different aspects of happiness raised in Chapter 7.

This has to do with the degree to which each option will give you the autonomy, mastery and sense of purpose that Daniel Pink discusses as well as looking at more practical matters such as which will pay more and which locations will cost more or less to live.

The chart includes a small calculation sheet to figure out your living expenses in a particular *place*. This reflection is located here, as opposed to the analysis of *place*, because the cost of living needs to be associated with the financial rewards that are possible in both the immediate and medium terms of different options.

G. Happiness

Options Leading combinations of Space, Role and Place			
Autonomy			
Mastery			
Sense of Purpose			
Short Term Financial Reward			
Medium Term Financial Reward			
Family			
Other _____			
Other _____			
Overall Rating			

Expenses	Monthly	Annual
Housing		
Transportation & Health Care		
Day to Day Living Expense		
Nice to Haves		
Savings		
Total Expenditure		

Evaluate each option with respect to each criteria using a simple scale ranging from - - - to + + + Avoid simply adding up the plusses and minuses as some criteria, such as family, might count much more than others.

Transitions

Chapter 8 discusses changing jobs during your professional life, and this chart is designed to help you reflect on where you are and what you may want to do.

The first part of the chart is designed to help you reflect on where you are in your current position. It draws on the ideas of Paddy Miller and his book Mission Critical Leadership explained in the box of Chapter 8. The basic question is how long you have been in your current combination of space, role and place and is it time for a change.

The second part is more focused on specific problems you may have with your current situation and whether it is time to quit.

H. Transitions

Current Position	Reflection
Average Days Multiply by no. of jobs by 365 and divide by years of experience	
MCL Phase 0 - 200 Opportunity; 200 - 500 Efficiency; 500 + Achievement	
Opportunity 1. Do you have a plan? 2. Are there quick wins? 3. Have you set expectations?	
Efficiency 1. Is the team strong enough? 2. Are the results sustainable? 3. Are the expectations reasonable?	
Achievement 1. Has your time been successful? 2. Do you have a successor? 3. What's next for you?	
Time Frame Consider how much time would be required to successfully complete the job and move on to the next job	

Reason to Quit	Don't Quit	Think About it	Quit
You feel you are underpaid compared to colleagues			
You have a better offer (more money or prospects)			
You are desperately bored at work			
You do not like your boss			
You do not like the CEO or Sr. VP			
You feel this is the wrong field of endeavor for you			
You have no clear mentor in the organization			
You do not see a path to a desirable future in the organization			
Your boss is abusive or unethical			
The organization allows abusive or unethical behavior			
Overall Reflection			

Purpose

This chart is designed to encourage you to think about your own purpose at this and the next phase in your professional life. The questions ask if the specific combinations you are looking at will allow you to be true to that purpose and what are the trade-offs that you may have to make.

I. Purpose

Question
How would you describe the primary purpose for the next phase of your life? Answers might involve making money to build financial security, solving a major problem, or exploring your own capabilities and interests.
How likely will the options you are pursuing allow you to be true to that purpose? This answer could have a degree of probability or perhaps indicate a need to re-think the options under consideration.
What steps or trade offs are required in the immediate term? Maybe the "dream job" is two or three steps away. What are the steps and why are they worth it?
Can you imagine another phase beyond this one perhaps with a different purpose and what would it be?

Education and training

In the case you do feel it is time to make a profound change, you may feel that
you need some additional training for the next phase, and this chart gives you
a place to list the different options you may have uncovered and compare them.

What makes this difficult is you may find yourself comparing courses and
programs which are very different from each other since education is undergoing a profound change.

J. Education & Training

Options				
Institution/ Company				
Description Describe the program under consideration looking particularly at the duration, format, location and other features such as: - Full / Part Time - Length (days, weeks) - face to face, on Line, or blended				
Cost Calculate the total program cost including the out of pocket tuition and expenses, the total time required and also the opportunity cost meaning lost revenue if you need to give up other paid work				
Timeliness Is the education timeless or does it respond to emerging trends and technologies?				
Relevance How directly applicable will the learning be for your next professional move?				
Fit Does the learning methodology fit with your own personality and style				
Overall Evaluation How does the opportunity compare to other, different alternatives for learning?				

Master plan

The last chart is there to help you chart out your next three of four moves in the next phase in your professional life or even the phase after that.

As discussed in Chapter 9, I do not recommend that anyone try to change the *space* they work in, the *role* they play and the *place* they work all at once unless they are independently wealthy or have been given the opportunity by someone they trust completely.

Instead, it might make sense for you to play a new role or go to a new location in the space you are currently in. Perhaps you can change another dimension in 12–18 months and then, in a few steps, make a complete transition.

K. Master plan

	Time Frame Years	Space	Place	Role
Starting Point How would you characterize your current situation ?				
Step 1 How would you change first ?				
Step 2 How would you change second ?				
Step 3 How would you change third ?				
Objective Where would you like to get to and when ?				

Of course, detailed plans over the course of many years normally do not work out exactly as we expect them to. I do believe in any case that thinking through such plans can give you a better sense of where you are going and why.

Conclusion

If there is one thing that 2020 and 2021 has made clear, it is that we are living in turbulent and changing times. In fact, I feel that we are at an inflection point in human history. We have, on the one hand, achieved amazing economic progress around the world, while, at the same time, are dealing with a number of large, complex problems that go from income inequality to resource scarcity and environmental challenges.

All of this in the face of the obvious risks to health as well as digitalization and geopolitical tensions.

What all of this says to me is that you should not assume that tomorrow will be the same as yesterday and ought to think about what the changing world means for your own professional career.

The purpose of the book is to give you a guide to do that.

I encourage you to learn what you can about the trends that are changing the world and drill down to what might impact you and your family.

Learn how to tell your own professional story so that you can share it with others and also as a way to lead into thinking about where you may want to go in the next step along your professional journey.

Think through what combinations of *role*, *space* and *place* appeal to you. I also suggest you do your best to look at this question over time and develop some scenarios for the future that you think are realistic. This allows you to test your choices and develop ideas which might be future proof.

Having clear ideas of where you want to go will help you get there regardless of whether you want to change a job within a phase of your professional life or are ready to move to a new phase all together.

Part of the overall story will involve receiving additional training, and this is natural in a changing and dynamic world.

My hope is by applying the principles in the book, you can chart a professional course which will give you the economic security you need as well as helping you to be happy and perhaps have a clear sense of purpose.

Key Ideas Chapter 12

- In changing phases or even jobs in our professional life, there is no excuse not to do extensive homework on the *space*, *role* and *place* you are considering.
- Working with people you trust over long periods of time can be especially rewarding and you may even follow certain people regardless of the *space* and *place* they choose to go.
- Getting advice from people you admire and respect can be invaluable although take care that you do actually listen to what they say.
- I strongly suggest writing down your ideas as you read through the different sections and chapters of the book and have provided a series of charts for that purpose.

FIGURES

.

BOXES

INDEX

CPSIA information can be obtained
at www.ICGtesting.com
Printed in the USA
JSHW020751060822
29006JS00001B/2

9 781839 985102